COERCED TO Courageous

TAKING BACK YOUR POWER AFTER COERCIVE CONTROL AND DOMESTIC ABUSE

STORIES OF STRENGTH AND SUCCESS

Compiled by KC Andrews

A catalogue record for this book is available from the National Library of Australia

 Formatted with Vellum

money or valuables, it is their safety, trust, self-confidence, well-being and potential.

It seems to be generally accepted that there are four stages to addressing domestic violence, namely, prevention, early intervention, crisis response and recovery. Whilst *Coerced to Courageous* relates primarily to recovery, it and its three predecessors also contribute to increased awareness of all aspects of domestic violence.

Coercive control is now being exposed in all its dark forms and there is hopefully an unstoppable momentum towards a future Australian society that is better, fairer and safer. There is still much to do though and a long way to travel before we are the country we should be.

The work of Broken to Brilliant, including this latest publication, is an important step in that journey. Finally, a special thanks to the ten women who shared their personal stories and whose courage, determination and resilience are an inspirational example for others to follow.

Bob Atkinson AO APM, *Co-Chair Domestic and Family Violence Prevention Council, Patron – Broken to Brilliant*

It is impossible to read *Coerced to Courageous* without feeling immense admiration for the women that have shared their stories. Each story provides such an honest and inspiring account of each woman's journey dealing with coercive control, and their courageous steps towards empowerment. At the end of each chapter, the authors provide the reader with words of hope, encouragement and advice for their own journey – an essential resource for those that may be currently experiencing domestic violence and providing a practical guide to healing and thriving.

The voice that the wonderful team at Broken to Brilliant has provided to survivors through this book (and those before it) is incredibly impactful. This is a resource that will most definitely provide comfort and hope to those who need it, as well as awareness of the real crisis that coercive control presents for so many of those around us. Thank you so much to all involved for the huge effort involved in publishing such a thoughtful and insightful read.

We support women at refuge, offering crisis accommodation when they are at their most vulnerable, fearful and lowest point. The agonising decision to leave their home, belongings, formal and informal supports is harder than most people understand because it is not just things they leave behind, it is that they know that their personal safety risk has now increased. Many women have lived in fear for so long and adjusted their behaviour to accommodate the perpetrator's often intentionally cruel, strategic and tactical behaviour, it has become the norm. More recently we have seen women use the term 'gaslighting', understanding this term and its associated behaviours – but Coercive Control is a newly coined term. We explain the nature of coercive control as ongoing, patterned behaviour perpetrated for the purpose of controlling another person. This book is a great resource that helps women easily understand that the behaviours they are experiencing are not acceptable and that they are experiencing domestic abuse. It assists women in understanding that each of the behaviours may not seem bad or significant individually, but all together, it's a systemic way of breaking their spirit and having power and control over them.

Kristen and Siti, *Chisolm Support Workers*

Chisolm Inc, Supporting Women & Children
escaping Family Violence since 1984

~

Rotary deals with humanitarian disasters daily. Domestic abuse is one of the worst, because of the trauma, disorientation and psychological stress it engenders. Unlike a natural disaster – awful as they are – nature in its wrath is indiscriminate. The violence towards a person is intentional and destroys trust and often faith in humanity; it is by definition evil. The pillar of love and trust, on which the holy ideal one built a true and trusting relationship, is suddenly shattered, with all the consequent disillusionment and horrors. Add the fact that some women need to continue nurturing young children and maintaining a degree of normalcy in the face of horrors and disorientation, and the burden of daily life can become intolerable.

The Rotary Club of Brookfield, Queensland 4069, fully aligned with the general humanitarian principles and the current programs of Rotary International, supports numerous domestic abuse initiatives throughout Queensland. We are proud to support Broken to Brilliant down the years for those survivors on the road to recovery.

It is instructive to read the feedback from women who have enrolled in the programs. That elusive inner transformation is necessary in order to tackle a new life entirely afresh and without old habits to draw one into another negative, abusive relationship. As one survivor emphasised, 'a caterpillar doesn't become a butterfly by simply growing wings – it must transform'. How true and poignant.

A healing process following trauma and disaster is both necessary and to be encouraged, and for this a variety of practical strategies are important – all utilised by Broken to Brilliant. The need for a role model is vital, as well as programs that emphasise a light at the end of the tunnel. An invisible transference or 'field' effect can gradually permeate a broken soul as well. Tapping into a positive group energy creates hope and optimism.

Many victims write of their personal experiences or break-throughs as epiphany or soul-level recovery. One survivor even mentions that 'the only place to be is in the present'. This contains a powerful mystical truth, for it dawns on many people at some stage in their lives that they had been living a largely constructed and conditioned mental ideal, a dead world. To grad-ually learn to live in the 'now' is a shape-shift of great significance for those on the road to recovery, because it connects and prompts them to live in the excitement of a fresh new dimension, so neces-sary if they are not to return to old habits and patterns. To quote a victim in their own words, 'it is the impermanence of these moments that makes these experiences so magical'. Once the veil of illusions gradually dissolves, survivors can reconnect with something far greater than themselves. Mental limitations are abandoned and a true, living presence can emerge from its hiber-nation. As one of the writers reported another survivor, 'I am so grateful for … the love living in my heart'.

Broken to Brilliant balance this invisible positive force along with practical and multi-disciplinary programs, ranging from advice on such matters as legal, housing and financial, as well as ensuring the victims are empowered through full awareness of these programs designed to help them.

Communication of these ideals and programs through aware-ness at all levels is therefore to be encouraged and supported.

G. TILLEY, Rotary Club Brookfield

This is not just another book.

It is coerced victims' voices, raw and vulnerable,
now finally heard.

It is courageous survivors' stories, unmasked, creating change
as they share their strengths and success.

May each word you read allow the brave, brilliant
and resilient you to emerge.

With each page you turn, may it guide you
to a new chapter in your life.

BOOK FEEDBACK SURVEY

Please complete the Broken to Brilliant book feedback survey.
We value your insights.

THANK YOU

These Courageous authors have reflected on their lives and dredged up the manipulation, coercion, lies, and the controlling ways.

They have shared their pain, shame, humiliation, and anger to help themselves and others understand the impact of coercive control.

Their heartfelt words will grip you and tug at your heart as you wonder how they kept going. They have come so far and turned their lives around. You will be inspired by each and every story.

We thank them for giving over 12 months of their time to bring this book to life. To shine a light behind the closed doors of abuse and also on the post-separation abuse that continues.

We thank each and every author in this fourth book for giving so much of themselves, their story and their time, to move themselves forward and help other survivors do the same. They have given so much without fame or recompense.

To each author, thank you for being brave, resilient and brilliant in sharing your story.

Each and every story of strength and success inspired us to complete this fourth book to help you on your journey and to 'pay it forward' to another survivor on their journey.

Without financial support we could not bring this book to life. Broken to Brilliant is thankful to have secured a $19,200 grant from The CM & JA Whitehouse Foundation.

This grant has funded author writing training, editing, proofreading, the printed book, and an ebook, as well as an audio book and podcasts to provide resources  in many forms to help rebuild the lives of people who have survived domestic abuse.

During the creation of *Coerced to Courageous* once again we put our 'pay it forward' model and mission into action. The four-day, live-in writing workshop was facilitated and supported by six authors and domestic violence survivors from our previous books (plus the Publishing Consultant) mentoring fellow survivors to create a new chapter in their lives. This helps survivors to recover, rebuild and heal after abuse.

The four-day, live-in workshop involves long days and we thank the writing workshop presenters and supporters:

- Belinda Pollard, Small Blue Dog Publishing
- Amber Johnson, art therapy, HEART Program leader and speaker
- Amber Woodford, Broken to Brilliant author, Blogging Self-Care presenter and speaker
- Sharon Le Fort, Broken to Brilliant author, Vision Board Program leader and speaker
- Jamie Shepherd, Mental Health First Aider, HEART Program Leader, Broken to Brilliant author and speaker
- Andrea Miller, Co-Founding Director Broken to Brilliant, author, Op Shop Manager and speaker
- Kate Smith, Founding Director Broken to Brilliant, author and speaker
- Woodlands of Marburg and their supportive, caring staff.

Also, thank you to:

- those who wrote a testimonial, reading the book in a short time frame and providing your heartfelt reflections
- the narrators who have donated their time and voices to the chapters of *Coerced to Courageous*. To ensure the anonymity and safety of each author we cannot list which chapter each voice artist narrated.
- those who have shared how our stories of strength and success have helped them. These are the words of encouragement that fuel our passion and dedication to bring this mosaic of healing to life.

FOREWORD

Coercive Control is an insidious thing. It is like a fog that permeates every area of your everyday life.

It creeps slowly across your relationship landscape and before you realise it, it's covering you. It's subtle, it's camouflaged, it's even wrapped up in what seems to be logical meaning.

It starts small – unrecognisable, really. An offhand, throwaway comment, a simple remark or even an act to help you do something 'the right way'. It could be a suggestion about what colour looks good on you or a hint highlighting a friend's 'rude' behaviour towards him.

He likes to know where you are and who you are with because he cares. He wants to spend more time with you because he likes to be with you. Then you are so busy doing things with him you no longer have time to see family and friends much. They slowly drift away as you are never available to catch up and you don't even realise how isolated you have become.

In time, he makes the decisions about pretty well everything so you 'don't have to worry'. He knows what's best about most things, even what you and the children do, what food you buy, what you should wear and if you should work outside the home.

He probably handles the finances as it really 'isn't your forte' and he has a better understanding of what's coming in and going out, anyway.

You are busy doing what he wants, when he wants, how he wants, because then everything will be fine, he won't get upset, he won't get angry, he won't yell at the kids and there won't be fights.

We all want to find our soulmate and have a perfect relationship, complete with diamond anniversary and walking hand in hand on the beach, still in love after all the years. We believe it is achievable as we have seen it in movies and read about it in books. We even know people who have this.

But for these courageous authors, their soulmate was more like checkmate. Trapped, with nowhere to go and no way out. Left wondering when the first bad move happened.

Leaving an abusive relationship is hard, really hard. And it doesn't just stop because you leave. It follows you. The chains of coercion and abuse have robbed you of your confidence, your family and friends, most likely your own finances, and even the ability to think you can make decisions on your own. And then of course there is the harrowing court system and possibly ongoing abuse, stalking, or worse by your ex.

It's also not easy to bare your soul on pages for the world to read. To step forward and recount the 'red flags' that went unseen or the friend that was hurt by your absence, and to admit to the effects of the trauma experienced that may even today still trigger you.

However, these resilient women have done just that. They are the Warriors Brave. The battle-worn soldiers who carry on despite the pain, in the hope that their story will provide camaraderie, self-belief, understanding and encouragement to others.

When you read their stories, spare a thought for the years they battled, the fight they fought to win the war that would bring them and their children happiness and peace. They have been wounded over and over, but have gathered their strength to relive their story one more time, to convey the true meaning of coercive control in its many forms and the part it plays in domestic and family abuse and violence.

These brave, resilient, brilliant authors have not only penned their years of coercive control and abuse, but they have written about what they have learnt and the tools that worked for them that they found helpful to rebuild their lives after abuse. The steps that helped them create a new chapter in their life – one of success, achievement and happiness.

I give praise for their courage for stepping forward. I pay homage to their bravery to write what they have been through. I applaud their post-abuse achievements. Most of all, I give heart-felt thanks for the difference their stories will make to every person who reads them, and for the ripples of confidence their stories will instil in fellow domestic abuse survivors, to provide encouragement to move out of the fog and create the life they deserve.

Andrea
Author, Trainer, Speaker
and Director of Broken to Brilliant

CONTENTS

INTRODUCTION

'I am a lot of things. Raw. Vulnerable. Sometimes I am not okay. No longer invisible. Determined. Nothing will hold me down. Today I feel like a star. Proud of who I am. Worthy, loved and resilient.'

As domestic violence survivors we knew only too well that there was limited support for our long-term recovery following coercive control and abuse. We were not going to stand for that. Something had to be done. You cannot stand back and expect that someone else will do what is needed. You need to step forward and be the change, to pay it forward, to give back and help others.

The charity Broken to Brilliant was legally established December 2015 and we launched our first book in May 2016. Broken to Brilliant was founded by domestic violence survivors to support and mentor fellow survivors to rebuild, recover and heal their lives after all forms of abuse. We do this by using our personal lived experiences. We develop and deliver a range of programs using narrative therapy, art therapy, and equine therapy to address psychological and emotional wellbeing, improve economic security, create connections, enhance recovery and generate post-traumatic growth. We share stories to shine a light on the complex road to recovery that lies ahead. We combine the survivor-mentor relationship, mutual rehabilitation, and story-telling into a pay-it-forward model, holding live-in writing work-shops and publishing stories of strength and success.

It is therapeutic for survivors to share their life story in a way that doesn't deny the trauma but also conveys their courage, determination, strength, and resilience. Reflecting on how far they have come and describing their survival and the steps and strategies they put in place to recover after adversity[1] empowers them. Voicing their personal experience through creative expression is a self-help tool[2] that can facilitate healing from the trauma of domestic violence.[3] Stories of survival, recovery and the rebuilding of oneself and life following violence and abuse is restorative.[4,5] Reclaiming the narrative power over their lives, redefining and reframing their experiences with a focus on strengths and resilience, aids the recovery journey.

Through our series of books sharing survivors' strength and success after violence and abuse we are creating heartfelt, powerful, genuine connections between survivors. They are forming a tribe and a village to share how to put together the pieces of the jigsaw-journey of rebuilding, recovering and healing. Our approach to each story – sharing the raw truth, the struggles and strengths, the solutions, as each survivor emerges to celebrate their power – restores hope for both the survivor and the readers.

WHAT IS COERCIVE CONTROL?

The theme of **Coerced to Courageous** is coercive control. The words may be new to the general community as coercive control laws are enacted in Australia and overseas, but domestic violence survivors have been living with and escaping from coercive control for years. Actually, coercion is part of the definition of domestic violence in the *Queensland Domestic and Family Violence Protection Act 2012*[6] and it is also in other domestic violence Acts across Australia.[7,8]

Coercive control has been occurring for decades, and indeed throughout human history. Perpetrators have not been held to account. This is evident when applications for domestic violence protection orders (or similar) are civil, not criminal, proceedings. Domestic violence does not become a criminal offence until the perpetrator breaches a domestic violence restraining order. We believe coercive control must be categorised as a criminal offence, to hold perpetrators to account for their actions. Broken to Brilliant made a submission to the Queensland Government supporting the introduction of coercive control laws based on feedback from survivors.

When we consulted with domestic violence survivors, they all expressed that the current laws and the application of those laws by police and the courts have not held perpetrators to account for their behaviour. They felt betrayed by the system and society; there was no justice and the legal process caused harm to themselves and their children.

Survivors felt that perpetrators got off scot-free.

Survivors shared that nothing happened to perpetrators for breaching restraining orders and committing these types of offences: stalking; rape; sexual abuse; showing children pornography; stealing; fraud; drugging their partners for sexual abuse; threats to kill; smothering; attempted drowning; non-lethal strangulation; break and enter; threatening letters and text messages; threatening to commit suicide; threatening to harm pets; harming the pets; destroying property; stealing property; hocking property; leaving flowers, notes or boxes of food; phone calls and voice messages; name calling; verbal abuse; controlling finances; and inciting fear. There were no consequences for the perpetrator even when all these ongoing behaviours were reported to the police. These actions are all examples of coercive control.

You cannot experience domestic violence without coercive control, as coercive control is at the core of all domestic violence.[9] **Coercive control** is a pattern of abusive behaviours against another person over time, with the effect of establishing and maintaining power and dominance over them. The abuse is a repeated pattern or cycle of behaviour that escalates over time, slowly eroding the victim's confidence and ability to leave.[10] Control is achieved through fear, violence or threatening behaviour.[11] In most cases, the offender is male and the victim female.[12,13]

Abusive behaviours that perpetrators can use as part of their pattern of abuse include:

- **Physical abuse** – includes direct assault on the body (strangulation or choking, shaking, eye injuries, slapping, pushing, spitting, punching, or kicking); use of weapons including objects; assault of children; locking the victim out of the house; sleep and food deprivation.
- **Sexual abuse** – any form of pressured/unwanted sex or sexual degradation by an intimate partner or ex-partner, such as sexual activity without consent; causing pain during sex; assaulting genitals; coercive sex without protection against pregnancy or sexually transmitted disease; making the victim perform sexual acts unwillingly (including taking explicit photos without their consent); criticising or using sexually degrading insults.[14]
- **Spiritual and religious abuse** – denial and/or misuse of religious beliefs or practices to force victims into subordinate roles; misuse of religious or spiritual

traditions to justify physical violence or other forms of
abuse.

- **Social abuse** – systematic isolation from family and friends through techniques such as ongoing rudeness to family and friends to alienate them; instigating and controlling a move to a location where the victim has no established social circle or employment opportunities; forbidding or physically preventing the victim from going out and meeting people.
- **Emotional abuse** – blaming the victim for all problems in the relationship; constantly comparing the victim with others to undermine self-esteem and self-worth; sporadic sulking; withdrawing all interest and engagement (for example, weeks of silence); emotional blackmail.
- **Verbal abuse** – swearing and continual humiliation, either in private or in public, with attacks following clear themes that focus on intelligence, sexuality, body image, and capacity as a parent and spouse.
- **Economic abuse** – complete control of all money, including forbidding access to bank accounts; providing only an inadequate 'allowance'; not allowing the victim/survivor to seek or hold employment; and using all wages earned by the victim for household expenses.
- **Psychological abuse** – driving dangerously; destruction of property; abuse of pets in front of family members; making threats regarding custody of any children; asserting that the police and justice system will not assist, support, or believe the victim; denying an individual's reality.
- **Reproductive coercion** – patterns of controlling and manipulative behaviours used to interfere with a person's reproductive health and decision-making.[15]

You are stopped from making choices about your menstrual cycle, sex and sexual pleasure, pregnancy, and birth.[16]

- **Lateral abuse** – organised, harmful behaviours that we do to each other collectively as part of an oppressed group. When people are consistently oppressed, they live with great fear and great anger and turn on those who are closest to them.[17]
- **Systems abuse** – manipulation of legal and other systems by perpetrators of family violence, done to exert control over, threaten and harass a current or former partner. They make complaints and applications through courts and Centrelink to delay, defer or prolong cases and to deplete the victim's financial status and cause emotional and psychological harm.
- **Technology facilitated abuse** – a broad term that refers to using mobile, online, and other digital technologies to abuse another person. These include harassing behaviours; image-based sexual abuse; monitoring and controlling behaviours using tracking devices or security cameras; emotional abuse and threats via social media, email and messaging services.
- **Animal abuse** – can involve hitting and/or kicking causing injury or death, or severe neglect leading to starvation.[18]

Coercive control also includes monitoring a victim-survivor's actions, restricting a victim-survivor's freedom or independence, and overall attacking and undermining the victim's autonomy and self-determination.

As you read each chapter in our series of books you will be dismayed by the coercive tactics used by perpetrators; they are akin to wartime torture techniques. Survivors have experienced the following from the perpetrator:

- telling them to remake the coffee, until they got it right, every day, for years
- threatening to commit suicide, and providing examples of how he has attempted it before when relationships ended
- lying to doctors about the victim's religious status so they cannot receive a life-saving blood transfusion
- using psychological warfare through name calling and constant verbal abuse
- controlling all the finances, so that they have to phone for funds to be transferred to the card, after he had checked what is being purchased
- forcing them into prostitution
- tell them they are putting on weight, controlling the food they eat and forcing them to exercise
- saying they are not being a good enough wife and making complaints
- not speaking to the partner for weeks, looking straight through them, while being gregarious with friends
- informing them that they do not really have any friends, that their friends are just using them
- hurting, kicking or verbally abusing their pets
- using the children to hurt the victim by restricting and withholding any medical attention or treatment for the children while in the perpetrator's care on shared parenting visits
- limiting the victim's ability to access any type of home care
- giving the victim medication or drugs that are not prescribed, such as sleeping tablets, tranquilisers or other drugs to enable sexual abuse

- taking sexual abuse photography and videos while the victim is drugged, then revealing the images and using these as threats to stop the victim from leaving or pursuing assault charges
- sending a deposit to their bank account; for example, 10c with an abusive message in the deposit description
- hurting children or putting children in dangerous situations, for example: not feeding them, driving fast with children in the car, withholding medication, locking their mother outside so breast feeding cannot be done while she can hear her child screaming to be fed
- taking the children away from the victim, thereby making the victim return to the perpetrator
- using the victim's mental health problems in affidavits in court, for example, contacting the victim's mental health professional to gain information to be used against the victim
- portraying themself as the victim's carer to get information, empathy and gain control of the situation and the victim
- using the legal system to financially ruin the victim
- using friends and family of the victim to spy on them and spread gossip while the abuser paints themselves as the victim.

RED FLAGS

You will read how survivors missed, dismissed, or rationalised away their behaviour – the abuser was just having a bad day! They struggle to recognise the signs of coercive control and domestic violence.

The signs have been named 'red flags' because we need to take notice of red flag behaviours and not be dismissive – these are warning you of a controlling, abusive person.[19,20,21,22]

This video from the Lady Musgrave Trust provides a useful interactive summary of key behaviours: https://thehandyguide.com.au/red-flags

Legal Aid NSW groups the behaviours into the following themes.[23]

Charming behaviours:

- they seem very thoughtful, considerate, caring, and understanding; you, your family and friends think they are wonderful.

Emotional abuse:

- continuous criticism and humiliation in front of other people
- emotional blackmail – for example, 'If you loved me, you would…'
- ignoring or refusing to talk
- losing their temper frequently over little things
- speeding the relationship up – quickly moving in together or opening joint bank accounts
- making you feel as if you are walking on eggshells to keep the peace
- playing mind games or making you feel guilty
- refusing to take responsibility for their actions – blaming you, drugs, or alcohol for their behaviour.

Controlling behaviours:

- monitoring what you are doing – going through your text messages, emails, and social media
- using technology to track where you are

- telling you to check in with them regularly
- telling you what to wear, where you can go, and who you can spend time with
- controlling how much money you have or preventing you from getting a job
- threatening you with weapons and/or to hurt or kill you, the children, family, or pets
- threatening to publish private information
- refusing to use birth control or protection
- jealousy – accusing you of having affairs.

Isolating behaviours:

- discouraging or preventing you from seeing family, friends, or work colleagues outside of work; isolating you from other people
- preventing you from practising religion
- encouraging you to spend more and more time with them
- moving you long distances away.

Physical abuse:

- shoving, pushing, tripping, pinching, spitting, hair pulling
- close-up, in-your-face screaming
- holding you down and ejaculating over you
- causing injuries such as scratches, bruises, and broken bones
- kicking or punching; hurting pets
- strangulation.

If you recognise these signs and behaviours, you need to get help from trained professionals who can work with you to keep you safe while you exit the relationship. Find help in the Contact Numbers section at the back of this book.

FAMILY AND DOMESTIC VIOLENCE STATISTICS

Despite awareness-raising campaigns, every country is battling the bane of domestic and family violence. The World Health Organisation reviewed data from over 161 countries and areas and found that worldwide, nearly one in three, or 30%, of women have been subjected to physical and/or sexual violence by an intimate partner or non-partner or both.[24]

Worldwide, the amount of family and domestic violence experienced is alarming.

- In the United States, an average of 20 people experience intimate partner physical violence every minute. This equates to more than ten million abuse victims annually.[25]
- In England and Wales, it is estimated that 2.4 million adults (1.7 million women and 699,000 men) – that is, approximately one in five adults aged 16 years and over – had experienced domestic abuse since the age of 16 years.[26]
- In Europe, one in three women have experienced some form of physical and/or sexual violence since the age of 15. One in two have experienced sexual harassment and one in ten have experience online harassment.[27]
- More than two-fifths (44%) of women 15–49 years of age in sub-Saharan African countries experienced some form of Intimate Partner Violence.[28]
- A fifth of all Russian women have been physically abused by a partner, and more than 12,000 women

died as a result of domestic violence in the 2011-2019 period.[29] In 2017, Russia decriminalised some forms of domestic violence.[30]

- In Asia, 16–55% of women report experiencing physical and/or sexual violence by an intimate partner in their lifetime.[31]

In Australia:

- men are more likely to experience violence from strangers and in a public place; women are most likely to know the perpetrator (often their current or a previous partner) and the violence usually takes place in their home
- one in six Australian women and one in 16 men have been subjected to physical and/or sexual violence
- emotional abuse is experienced by one in four women and one in six men
- one in five women and one in 20 men have experienced sexual violence (sexual assault and/or threats)
- one woman is killed every nine days and one man is killed every 29 days by a partner
- almost one in three hospitalisations for assault injury are due to family and domestic violence.[32]

THE IMPACT OF FAMILY AND DOMESTIC VIOLENCE

The impacts of coercive control and domestic violence can be life-long. We are yet to see the full impact for those that endured increased contact with their perpetrator during COVID-19 lock-downs, stay at home orders, reduced social interactions, and being subjected to increased monitoring.[33]

For those who have shared their story in our books, they have left the abusive relationship for between one year and more than 20 years ago. Yet their psychological scars are palpable.

When you leave, everyone thinks it stops and life goes back to normality quickly. This is not the case. Some leave safely, and the abuse stops. For most, the abuse escalates and continues after they have left and can continue for years. Victims are being dragged back to court 10–15 years post-separation as the abuser uses the legal system to continue their abuse and to financially cripple.

Somewhere along the recovery journey, there comes a time when you can stop, breathe, and think. This is when you are out of survival mode and you can start to unravel. As your mind is no longer controlled with ensuring you meet their every whim, you have time to think and reflect. You begin to realise the significant impact that coercive control and domestic and family violence has had on you and your children.

It erodes your and your children's self-confidence, self-esteem and self-identity and affects your everyday life, health and wellbeing, and your dreams and goals. The life you once knew – your home, your friends, your children's school, your sporting, social and spiritual life – GONE.

What most people do not understand is that escaping from coercive and abusive relationships can cause survivors to be overcome by an enormous sense of grief and loss. Their experiences can lead to depression, anxiety, and a range of other mental and physical health issues.[34] Research has found that the physical and mental health of women who had experienced domestic violence was 'consistently worse' after 16 years than those who had not experienced abuse, and these effects can last a lifetime.[35]

How long do we continue to tolerate the abuse? The #MeToo movement brought a global awareness to sexual abuse and created a sense of safety for survivors to share their stories. Society was more empathetic, and more perpetrators were held to account. We are on the precipice of another global change as coercive control laws are implemented. We must maintain this momentum of change.

No societal change will occur, however, unless everyone of all ages works together through RESPECTFUL relationships to break the violence. Every crevice in our society's systems, organisations, and workplaces needs change at the core.

Respectful

Relationships
Emotionally
Supportive
Positive
Enriching
Caring
Togetherness
Friendship
Understanding
Love

BROKEN
to Brilliant

We need more than a policy polish, a strengthening of legislation and action. We need a deep, cultural, heartfelt, radical change and transformation of our society now. Until this change occurs, the vines of violence will weave through our lives and society, ripping apart the fabric of family and our future.

What do you want for your family, friends, and the future?

THE IMPACT OF OUR SERIES OF BOOKS

There has been a gap in research on the post-abuse journey. How do survivors of domestic violence fully achieve psychological and physical wellbeing as they encounter the demands of creating a new life?[36,37,38,39]

The Royal Commission into Family Violence (2016) found that the 'current responses to family violence do not sufficiently emphasise recovery and restoration and may even impede it. The ultimate objective of the family violence system must be that victims, including children, can recover and thrive at their own pace.'[40]

Helping fellow domestic violence survivors in their journey after domestic violence is something we undertake from the knowledge of our lived experience: survivors mentoring fellow survivors. Until recently, there has been little known about the coping strategies used by survivors post abuse. As survivors, we knew this, and we have been sharing our journeys. By being brave and delving into our stories, reflecting on our strengths and resilience, we have shared the steps to rebuilding life after coercive control and domestic violence in four books. Across this series we have so far given a voice for 42 survivors to be heard.

Each time we commence our narrative therapy program, we receive more applicants' stories than we could fit into one book. For some survivors, they were still in unsafe situations and their journey was still too raw. Is there a right time? An exact number of months or years to be able to share your story? No, time is not the key factor. Readiness to share your story means being ready to do the hard work.

Can you recover after trauma and abuse? 'Recovery is not defined by the complete absence of thoughts or feelings about the traumatic experience but being able to live with it in a way that it isn't in control of your life.' [41] Recovery is unique to each survivor. The process is an ongoing journey of survival, of finding 'self' and becoming free from the fear and suffering caused by the trauma of abuse.[42] The journey of surviving and thriving occurs over time; it is chaotic, emotional, and unique to each person. As survivors, our stories share a resemblance in the steps taken to rebuild, recover and heal – though each person walks their rollercoaster route their own way.

BROKEN TO BRILLIANT

In 2016, we proudly launched our first book in this series, *Broken to Brilliant: Breaking Free to be You After Domestic Violence – Stories of Strength and Success*. Through generous donations to our 'Give a Book' campaign and through grants, thousands of these books have been gifted to domestic violence survivors in shelters and refuges, or to other services that support domestic violence survivors as they rebuild their lives.

Are these stories beneficial? Our survey found that readers said the book was inspiring and helpful. It educated them about domestic violence and strategies to rebuild lives. Most readers reported that they experienced personal growth after reading this self-help book.

We received encouraging words, such as: the book 'gives hope to others experiencing domestic violence and the choices they can make to have a new beginning'.

The ten *Broken to Brilliant* writers said they would recommend the writing process to other survivors, as they found that writing their story helped to turn a bad experience into a good one. It gave meaning to their experience, set them free and helped them to focus on the positives of what they had achieved. Knowing their story was going to serve others in the same situation made the process humbling and added a sense of purpose and worth to their lives. They felt honoured to be involved.

> 'It showed me that there was value to my life and my story and that I can turn my pain into purpose to help serve others.'

The book received a bronze award in the self-help category of the eLit award, a global program committed to illuminating and honouring the very best of English language digital publishing. The book also won the Author Elite Award in the Advice category.

The Author Elite Awards are bestowed for literary merit and publishing excellence in the writing and publishing industry.

TERROR TO TRIUMPH

The book *Broken to Brilliant* had a positive impact on people's lives — it breathed hope into people's hearts and inspired the spark of a new chapter in their lives. These stories created ripples of recovery and repair.

We could not turn away and stop these ripples of healing. And so, the concept for *Terror to Triumph* emerged.

We wanted to enhance our support for the authors, so this time we held a three-day, live-in writing retreat. Eleven women and one man attended. Activities included art therapy, writing techniques, exercise, meditation, and positive affirmation. The activities helped participants recover their ability to play, plan, laugh, create, hope, and write.

The authors said that the support we provided felt authentic, they felt loved, valued, and heard, which built trust among the group. The retreat changed them and their thinking. They left feeling more confident, encouraged, and open to alternative self-care methods. One person said,

> 'I leave a different person. There is no doubt about that.'

From the workshop, they were able to reconnect with their stories in a way that enabled them to focus more on what they had overcome and achieved in rebuilding their lives, rather than what they had experienced during the abuse. This enabled a clearer expression and understanding of the strategies survivors implemented as part of their rebuilding process.

Twelve brave authors stepped forward to share their stories of the terror experienced, the practical steps taken on their recovery, and how they reclaimed self to reach a sense of triumph.

> 'I had an overwhelming sense of belonging, which was both uncomfortable but welcomed.'

SHATTERED TO SHINING

Once again, we were inspired to embark on another book, due to the amazing breakthroughs the authors reported as a result of the *Terror to Triumph* writing retreat and sharing their stories.

Thanks to a grant from the Community Banking Sector, which provided funds for the publishing costs of the print, audio, and eBooks, the charity was able to call for author applications for *Shattered to Shining*. Reading their stories, you will gain a connection to each of the authors, as they share their story and their pain of being shattered from abuse, and their relief and aliveness as they shine again.

It was a profound pleasure to meet the brave, resilient authors at the *Shattered to Shining* four-day, live-in writing workshop. After this packed weekend, all authors agreed that the activities were helpful, useful, worthwhile, supportive, and well organised and facilitated. What they said they found most valuable about the workshop was that it offered different healing modalities such as writing, art, music, exercise, meditation, and group sharing. There were connections made, with no judgement. So much support was provided by the facilitators.

The experience of bringing their stories to life was a roller-coaster ride of oscillating emotions, from the depths of despair for the pain they endured to the elation at how they are now shining bright. In an author's words:

> 'I'm so grateful to have the opportunity to pour my story into words to help others! I hope it does! As I edited it and did the final read, I imagined someone reading it – just one person – and as they close the pages they think, "Okay, I'm going to get started!"
>
> Get started on your journey away from abuse – there is a world of happiness shining brightly for you to join.'

COERCED TO COURAGEOUS

The pandemic impacted our book publishing. We had planned to write a book with a group of interested survivors with professional backgrounds in Western Australia. We had also planned to go to Tasmania to write a book on recovery using spirituality and faith. Lockdowns and border closures stopped those plans.

Through a grant from the Trustees and Grants Review Panel of the Whitehouse Foundation we were able to continue our mission of sharing stories of strength and success to help survivors rebuild their lives.

Ten courageous authors immersed themselves into the narrative therapy writing process over ten months. There has been technical writing training on Zoom, writing exercises, and a four-day, live-in writing workshop. These courageous authors unmasked their inner selves and spilt their stories of sheer hell upon the pages. They are warrior women, taking back their power, breaking the chains of coercive control, letting their kaleidoscope of colour and creativity emerge. They celebrated taking back their power. Not in a boastful or fake way. But through real genuine connections. They felt seen, believed, safe and better as they found their tribe and began building a village of support.

This is their feedback about their discoveries from our author program.

'It has been an interesting and cathartic journey writing my story and it has lifted a burden I did not know I was carrying. I knew it would be therapeutic, but the benefits have been greater than I could have imagined. The retreat was one of the best experiences of my life and has changed the direction I was going, from being a prisoner to finding myself, forgiving my failings and dropping the anger and bitterness for the perpetrator and the broken patriarchal systems. The Broken to Brilliant authors' program has given me hope and a supportive circle of friends to sustain me on my new adventure. I am dancing with happiness and embracing my learnings through this healing journey.'

'I'm off to rejoice, my feelings floating off on a Zephyr high. Thank you for believing in me…'

'Every single part was well thought out, supportive, with great attention to detail.'

'Broken to Brilliant workshop was the most healing I've done in many years.'

'Connection with all the QUEENS here, valuing myself more, the writing workshops.'

'I can't possibly express how grateful I am for the experience and opportunity to be part of this creation alongside you and all of the amazing women. Thank you for your support, encouragement, and inspiration.'

'I feel lighter, freer and I am walking further.'

Be raw, be vulnerable, unmask You. Walk the path of the warrior women. Their courageous steps will lead you on a healing journey.

CHAPTER 1
CHOOSING ME

'I chose me and I will keep choosing me for the rest of my life. I'm worth choosing.'

As I sit here in this big white outdoor bathtub, I take a deep breath, inhaling the floral smells of the bubble bath and noticing just how at peace I feel. The water is cool on my skin, a relief from the hot climate, as I look out into the dense, dark green of the Daintree Rainforest on the first day of my holiday.

My first solo holiday.

After everything I've been through, I pinch myself to make sure this is real. I suddenly see the vivid blue of a Ulysses butterfly and I feel a thrill run through my body at this symbol of transformation.

You wouldn't recognise me from 18 months ago, when it all happened...

Leaving the man I'd spent almost 20 years of my life with was a hard, scary decision.

A decision my heart had been wanting to make for many years.

I agonised over it. I worried about my beloved cogs. I worried about where I'd live and how we could possibly pack up the house – there was so much stuff everywhere in the yard and garage. I even worried that I'd be throwing away 20 years of my life!

Mostly, I was terrified of what he might do and how he might act if I left him. I recognised this as a massive red flag and had done so for some time, but I was so scared, and for good reason.

The threat of suicide was real and present. He'd previously told me of a suicide attempt when an earlier relationship of his had ended. The threat was always underlying when he escalated his verbal attacks. Once, he'd actually described how he was going to kill himself – very calmly, in great detail. It's not an exaggeration to tell you I was held hostage by his threats.

I mean, how on earth could I possibly live with myself if he killed himself?

I'd been reading a book, *Too Good to Leave, Too Bad to Stay* by Mira Kirshenbaum. When I got to the chapters on power and humiliation, I knew.

I'd known for a very long time I didn't deserve his treatment. I felt like I was leading a small, compressed life, when I really wanted to live an expansive, free life.

When I read those chapters, I finally admitted to myself what I'd been denying: that I was trapped in a cycle of abuse. Shocking as this was, I knew I could no longer ignore or push this fact aside. My love and respect for myself had grown and I couldn't unknow what I now knew.

This knowledge didn't change the fact that I was as scared as f___.

I did the maths and decided within myself that I could afford the mortgage on my own. This made me feel more at ease with the practicalities of living. I started to imagine how life could be for me… and it felt good.

Leaving him felt possible for the first time.

In the moments that followed my decision, I felt pure freedom. It was the right decision for me. But it was quickly followed by great fear as to how he would react.

~

It was a clear, sunny December day. It was my favourite time of year, with the poinciana trees I loved coming into bloom, Christmas decorations at the shops, cicadas chirping at dusk. It was usually my favourite time of year… but not this year.

After all, I'd made *that* decision.

Standing at the kitchen table, my voice shaking, I said the bravest words I have ever said: 'I want to separate.'

I chose *me* for the first time in 20 years.

I want you to know that even with the horror that unfolded over the next three days and the trauma it caused me, I would NEVER go back and change my decision. NEVER.

My worst nightmare came true...

He killed himself.

~

For almost 20 years, I'd kept myself alive in a hostile, volatile environment by controlling myself and staying hypervigilant to this man's moods and needs.

I tiptoed on eggshells around him, a man who told me he loved me and showered me with affection while restricting my freedom and tearing my confidence to shreds. Coercive control, as I now know it to be. Insidious and violent, this type of abuse is damaging in a way I can't accurately describe. It's like he took my

26-year-old self and slowly tore her down over time, until my true essence could no longer be found.

I lived in a false reality where I believed that fear and intimidation was love. That abusive behaviour was normal. Where I acted outside of myself, all to stay safe and have as much peace as I could. The worst part was I didn't even realise I was caught in a cycle of abuse.

Firstly, there were 'the rules'. Rules I never agreed to. Rules that were unspoken. Rules that changed. Rules that slipped in so subtly over many years. Rules that were disastrous to break.

Couldn't look at my phone 'too much'. Not allowed male friends. Couldn't spend too much time with friends and family. Couldn't get home from work late. Not even 15 minutes. Getting stuck in traffic would cause my heart to beat fast with fear at the thought of what I'd cop if I was late.

I could go on an occasional girls' night out and the work Christmas party; however, there were always consequences, which included lecturing me on drinking, what I was wearing, accusations I was trying to attract other men, and questions about who would be there and what time I would be home.

We usually socialised together so he could make sure I wasn't doing anything outside of 'the rules'. Of course, I tripped up time and time again. Greeting a friend too enthusiastically, chatting to someone too long, hugging someone, staying out too late, wearing the wrong clothes (either too conservative or too slutty).

Celebrations and fun times were ruined. My birthday seemed to be his favourite day to see me in tears, often by picking a fight or insulting me. There were humiliating public fights. The time he caused a scene at a friend's fortieth. The time he drunkenly tried to run in front of traffic on a main road. The time I had to leave a work conference early because he was harassing me with phone calls and accusing me of having another man in my room. The ice-cold looks that would send a shot of pure terror through me and I knew I'd be in for a sleepless night of his ranting and raving when we got home.

Then there was the name calling, constant criticism and so-called 'jokes'. Being called a 'bitch' and given the finger was an everyday occurrence. Dinner being late, kitchen a mess, terrible cooking, washing not folded, ugly clothes, too sexy clothes, unattractive and fat, wasting money on the gym… and on and on.

Violently tickling me while I attempted to eat dinner; turning all the lights off before purposefully frightening me, knowing I am scared of the dark; measuring the distance between my nipple and belly button to see how much my breasts had sagged in the time we'd been together. Hilarious…

Then there were his moods, swinging between being overly attentive to cold treatment and screaming in my face. I honestly never knew what the conflict was about most of the time, when his yelling and ranting would begin. When I attempted to escape, he would follow me around the house, banging down closed doors to continue his rampage. It was always my fault, of course. And afterwards, it was up to me to apologise if I wanted peace – which I did, as I was desperate for relief from him.

He insisted on touching me in ways that revolted me, sex when I didn't want to have sex, painful sex acts that I hated. When I said no, he persisted, intimidated me until I gave in or, if I refused, he would just go ahead anyway or punish me with insults and yelling.

Behaviour I would never have accepted in the first year had just become my norm by the twentieth year. I lied to myself over and over, telling myself that this time would be the last time, then forgiving him over and over.

Oh, the shame I felt for staying.

IN THE WEEKS and months that followed the suicide, I was mostly numb. I couldn't feel anything at times.

I wish I knew then what I know now. That being numb is a valid feeling. Not being able to feel anything was my body's amazingly beautiful way of protecting me from unbearable horror and pain. Numbness helped me do hard things, like organising his funeral and even delivering the eulogy. But I judged myself for my numbness at the time and, later, when the numbness wore off, I grasped at anything I could to numb the pain, to escape seemingly unbearable emotions and the reality that was now my life.

I suffered flashbacks straight out of a horror movie, triggers that could send my whole central nervous system into overdrive in an instant. Anxiety and panic attacks were a daily occurrence. I felt emotions I never knew existed. Emotions that were so painfully unbearable, I couldn't stand to be myself.

I used anything I could to numb the pain. Drugs, alcohol, sex, shopping, food, risk-taking activities. I had little regard for my wellbeing. I self-medicated with wine every day for almost a year. Some days, I was in such a heightened, anxious state I would just watch the time turn to 4.00 pm (or 3.00 pm) before I would have a glass (or a bottle) of wine.

I started to face the hard truth that numbing painful emotions wasn't helping me. It was hurting me. Drinking bottles upon bottles of wine seemed like an easy escape, but the drunken meltdowns and hangovers that were full of self-loathing told me otherwise.

I needed to find a different way. But how did I even begin to deal with myself? Deal with the shame, the guilt, the trauma, the despair?

So I searched… and I searched… and I found that different way.

It wasn't what everyone told me: talk therapy and a belief that the healing would take the rest of this lifetime. It was different – it was deep and truly transformative. I took the crap that happened to me and used it. A caterpillar doesn't become a butterfly simply by growing wings. It literally breaks itself down and transforms every part into a completely new being.

Let me tell you about how I transformed into the incredible woman I am today.

I looked within and found I truly desired freedom, joy and peace. So, once again, I chose myself.

I chose to heal. And it is a choice.

Choosing to heal isn't easy. It's not smooth. It doesn't mean the pain just disappears. It involves looking within, doing the deep inner work, surrendering that which is numbing you from who you truly are.

It's both painful and beautiful, and totally worth it.

MY CENTRAL NERVOUS system is being triggered – that familiar wash through my body, followed by an intense sadness and anxiety. My heart is beating out of my chest. I go into the garden, put on some music, and just sit. I hug myself tight, allow the tears to fall, and feel the intensity of the emotions. I touch the deep, dark pain within and feel her – the rage, the despair, the shame. I am her. I can no longer reject her.

I accepted myself completely that day, the light and the dark within.

I've learned to be with my emotions. To embody them and feel them in full is the only way through them. It doesn't make the dark emotions any easier, but no longer rejecting them is a radical act of self-love. It's freedom.

Profound growth happens when you're in the darkness. When you're screaming in your car or lying on the ground sobbing. Seriously, the only thing that got me through some of the dark times was telling myself they would end. That, actually, the good emotions don't last either. The only place to be is in the present.

Even though my abuser was dead, the abuse continued. I had 20 years of training after all…

The voice in my head was judgemental and critical, and I held myself to ridiculously high standards. I had a long list of daily wellbeing practices, and while they were healthy habits, I wasn't doing them out of self-love. I was doing them out of self-loathing, trying to change myself and not believing I was good enough.

With the help of a coach, I started to be gentler with myself. I learned to tune the needs of my body, mind and soul. I ask myself, 'What do I need today?' and, 'How can I show myself more kindness?' I reframed the negative thoughts that came into my mind by asking myself what I'd say to a friend.

I had support from an amazing Trauma Therapist who taught me that trauma gets trapped in the body. No amount of talking or positive affirmations can shift trauma from within our body. We need to move through our emotions to process them.

I have found that the less I get my mind involved, the more effective the method. There is so much research and evidence about somatic therapy (mind/body connection) in healing trauma. While I believe talk therapy has its place and has helped me, it has been breathwork, tapping, body movement and energy work that have truly healed me.

The most powerful healers are available to us freely and easily. A walk in nature can take me from an anxious and overthinking state to calmness and clarity. I found beautiful forest areas in my big city that I never knew existed. My morning forest hikes grounded me and calmed me like nothing else. Nature is the most powerful healer.

Our breath is something we have available to us all of the time and I am beyond grateful that I discovered breathwork. I have released trauma and grief from deep within my body through breath, leaving me with feelings of joy and freedom. You cannot imagine the simplicity and power of the breath until you try it. Just take five deep breaths to your belly and notice how you feel afterwards. (p.s. group breathwork sessions are amazing!)

I worked with an Energy Coach I knew and trusted to release trauma memories from my body and subconscious mind. I had one session with her, and my daily panic attacks and anxiety attacks literally stopped overnight. She taught me tapping (EFT) and I now use this regularly to help quickly release negative emotions.

To discover who I am and take my power back, I've taken a deep look at my own patterns of behaviour. An anxious attachment style and co-dependent tendencies made me vulnerable to becoming caught in a cycle of abuse. My beautiful values of love, loyalty, kindness and forgiveness kept me there.

It is pure freedom to choose to own and love all aspects of myself, even the parts that got me into that mess!

What I do know about myself now is how strong I am. I have faced emotions I never knew existed and have experienced the darkest of the dark and survived. It's been 18 months since I chose myself that day and ended the abuse. It seems like a long time because I have come so far in my recovery, and yet, it's really only the blink of an eye.

I don't think I'll ever be a regular person. I don't even know what a 'normal' existence would be like. And that's totally okay, because I am extraordinary.

From me to you, and I want you to listen carefully to this… I took a massive leap of faith in myself when I made the decision to leave. I was terrified. I didn't know what would happen to me, if I'd ever be happy again. It was the best thing I ever did. Trust me when I say my life is not just better now, it has completely transformed into a life I could only have dreamed of.

Love fills every corner of my life, from my family and friends to all the experiences I have. I can do whatever I want now! I've started my own business, I take pole dancing classes, practise yoga, go out for dinners with friends, enjoy weekends away and lots more.

I know myself at depths I never knew existed. I make healthy choices for my body, mind and soul, truly honouring all parts of me. I choose not to use any external substance to numb my emotions, even the difficult ones, including alcohol, drugs and food. (Alcohol free for six months now!)

I have taken my power and freedom back in full.

It's a clear, sunny day and a gentle breeze is playing with my hair as I walk onto the tarmac. The sight of the bright red helicopter causes my stomach to flutter. I've never been on a helicopter before! It's the last leg of my holiday and I'm headed to the beautiful North Queensland outback.

I catch a glimpse of the ocean as the helicopter ascends before turning inland, and the terrain turns brown as we fly over the mountains. My nerves turn to pure gratitude for the life I'm now living. I deserve this happiness and joy.

I chose me and I will keep choosing me for the rest of my life.

I'm worth choosing.

CHOOSE YOU

You can also choose you. It is not an easy choice; we are conditioned to always consider others' needs first, before our own, especially when living in an abusive relationship. Through doing the deep inner work, you too can emerge from the suffocating cocoon of coercive control and be transformed and free to spread your beautiful wings. It is your choice. Will you choose you?

C—Choose you: Make a plan to focus on you and your healing. Recreate connections with family and friends.

H—Healthy healing: Acknowledge unhealthy use of external numbing agents such as medication, alcohol, drugs, excessive shopping or seeking out sexual partners. Focus on healing by making healthy choices for your body: healthy foods, exercise, sleep.

O—Outdoor activities: The outdoors aids in healing as nature has a calming effect over the body. Spend time in a leafy green park or go on a bush walk. Taking in the beauty of nature can create a sense of awe, amazement, wonder, admiration and respect. This will help to reduce stress, anxiety and depression, and helps with healing after trauma.

O—Our breath: Our own breathing can help reduce anxiety and stress. Your breath can be used to calm yourself when you are triggered. Breathwork can help heal trauma. Breathing techniques to try:

- Box breathing, also known as 4–4–4–4: Breathe all the air out of your lungs counting to four, hold for four, breathe in for four and hold for four.
- Soothing sigh: breathe in deeply, hold, breathe out with a sigh, relax your neck and shoulders, and repeat four times.

S—Somatic therapy: Somatic therapy includes the mind, body, spirit, and emotions in the healing process. Past trauma can be trapped within the body and be released by a body centred approach and mind-body exercises. The following therapies can also help – seek out a therapist who can guide you in the use of Tapping, also known as Emotional Freedom Techniques (EFT), and eye movement desensitisation and reprocessing (EMDR). You can try tapping yourself by using tapping videos. You can also try yoga, dancing, singing, running, and many other ways that you find work for you.

E—Emotions: Learn to be with your emotions. Recognise and name your emotions. Allow them to flow through. Embody them, feel them, integrate them, and accept them in full. Doing this is the only way through them. It doesn't make the dark emotions any easier, but no longer rejecting them is a radical act of self-love. It's freedom. Do this with support of a therapist.

For a downloadable PDF of the checklist above, go to <u>brokentobrilliant.org/coercedtocourageous</u>

CHAPTER 2
FAITH GAVE ME STRENGTH

'I have learnt that life is precious, and I enjoy the simplest of things these days. I have suffered, endured, dreaded and survived, and now I have a future that is free to be me. I can do anything, and I am finally free.'

I absolutely adored my husband with everything I had within me. I believed in him and trusted him to know better than me. I relied on his guidance to correct me when I made many unknowing mistakes.

When we were dating, my love would make us coffee. We would sit together at our outside table in the freshness of the morning, discussing his plans for us for the day. I started putting the kettle on to make our coffee for these times, and I felt so comfortable and at ease to do so.

One day when I was about to pour the water, he corrected me and showed me that I was to hold the jug at a certain height. Day by day I practised, till I could do it exactly the way he wanted. Then he screamed that we never made coffee that way and my coffee lesson started again.

Then it was the same for everything I did.

When he first showed me how to wash up, I thought he was just quirky and liked things done his way. It was such a small thing that I didn't mind changing, but then it was like this with all things. My kind gesture was me losing myself and him having total control.

HE TOLD me I had to leave my job as he was unwell. I worked for him at home with his business which was physical, dirty and completely under his constant surveillance. Somehow, in between, I had to keep maintaining the usual household chores and set up a nice lunch for him. I miraculously managed, and was able to do it all out of my never-ending source of love for him.

I received no pay. Once a month, I would ask for money so I could go to an op shop and buy items that I would then wash, fix and sell to have money to buy gifts for friends or family occasions.

If friends came over, I enjoyed cooking for them, but he would tell me that they didn't like my food and were rude to him. I could never imagine my friends doing or saying such things, but I noticed that they never came back. I quickly became isolated and thought maybe it was all true.

MY DAYS WOULD USUALLY START AROUND 4.30 am, when my husband would flick me on the head to wake me up. If I reacted, he would laugh. If I tried to ignore him, he would continue to flick me harder, or twist and pull my skin until I cried.

Each morning, I would water my vegetable and flower gardens. I would pretend that it was an annoyance, just so he would tell me to stay there longer. I learnt to stand looking annoyed, but inside I absolutely loved being in this beautiful space, thinking of what I could do to impress my husband on that day. I truly loved him, and each day I prayed while watering that our lives would change.

We lived on a property, and I was to keep it immaculate. At times I would ask if I could clean out a shed or do another hard job which would take me a couple of days, so I could be working alone at my own pace without him ordering me or watching me. Sometimes this backfired and he would help me, so we would be working together on the hard job till it was completed.

I really pressed into my Christian faith for peace, but my husband would curse God and scream that I was not to have beliefs in our home. I knew that if he feared my relationship with a God that could not be seen, I clearly had nothing I could do without his permission.

IT WAS NEARING Christmas and I asked my husband if we could go to the op shop so I could buy some gifts and decorations. To my surprise, he said that I could go alone. I tried to maintain my normal expression, but I was bursting with excitement inside to be given some free time alone.

As I got in the car, my husband kissed me goodbye and told me that he would open the gate for me to leave. He came to my car window and started to chat about my car, and then he found some dust on it and said I should wait so he could clean it. I sat waiting while he cleaned the outside of the whole car as I didn't dare move. He then popped the bonnet and checked the oil. I started to get anxious, trying to read his mood.

He asked me to check my car blinkers to see if they were working, but at that moment my mind overloaded and I couldn't remember where the blinker was. He reached into the car, looking closely at me, and breathed out a sigh which made me flinch, all while he pointed to the blinker.

He slowly stood back, watching me. He smirked, with his head tilted to the side, like he was proud that he had finally achieved his goal of scaring me out of my mind, and with such little effort. I had been so conditioned through abuse in every way that I knew I needed him to help me. I was no longer the capable, confident woman that he had first met.

My husband was restrictive with money. He said we had so many bills that I should happily go without. I sold second-hand items that I had fixed to get some small amounts of cash, but he always put his hand out, took the money, and said he would generously give me half. He bought many high-end vehicles in cash, and I was left questioning my sacrifices. He would at times show me huge wads of money that he was putting in odd places around our property, but when I looked for the money in mad moments, to escape, it had been moved. It was all a game for him to show control.

Any rare times that I was allowed to run errands alone, I was given a debit card with a zero balance, so that he would have to transfer money into it. I had to give him all the receipts.

When I dared to question if I could have money or why we didn't have a joint debit card, he said there were too many accounts with the business. He yelled that he gave me everything I needed, and continued to growl that I was selfish, fat, lazy and a slur of filthy swear words.

One early morning I was unwell, screaming in pain. He told me to wait until the medical centre opened. I could barely breathe, let alone talk, the pain was so intense. I waited as long as I could, then texted a family member to call me an ambulance. I went in the ambulance by myself, and my family met me at the hospital. I was told I needed emergency surgery.

My family waited with me for hours, but then I told them to go. 'My husband will be here soon.'

Later, when I was being wheeled to theatre, I called him. 'Why didn't you come? I'm scared. I've never had an operation before.' He told me vulgar sexual acts he liked and said I should keep that in mind, then laughed and hung up.

I was so hurt, I hoped to die during the operation, as I felt worthless and so sad. I regretted telling my family to leave the hospital when I needed love and support. I made excuses to them as to why he never showed up.

I left my husband several times, but he would promise to change. I would go back after a night or two. He would threaten to commit suicide, so I would rush back to take care of him in his fragile state.

I was so stressed, blood clots would come out of my nose. I tried to hide this because if he saw my nose bleeding he'd scream at me, 'Stop it, you're disgusting.' His eye would twitch as he swore and said vulgar things.

At times my headaches were so severe I put icepacks on my head, but only after he was asleep. If he woke before me and saw the ice packs, he would scream and swear at me all day. 'You are so mental, you have so many problems in your head, you're making yourself sick.'

One good day when I felt relaxed, sitting chatting nicely with him, he got up and slapped me hard across the face. As I struggled off the floor he was smirking, and I felt dead inside.

He suggested we have dinner by the fire for something nice. I couldn't answer straight away. His face became red and distorted while he screamed that I was slow. He spat on me several times, dragged me up the stairs, threw me on the bed while calling me names, and violently raped me.

Shocked and shaking, I waited till he fell asleep. I crawled out of the house, terrified he would wake up and catch me.

I could never bear to go on our property again. I was diagnosed with PTSD (post-traumatic stress disorder).

My initial first step was going to Centrelink. A compassionate staff member saw that I had no money in my bank and hadn't for many years, and I was given a crisis payment. I cried when they said I was homeless. They had a counsellor onsite who listened to me talk about my situation and called DV Connect for me.

DV Connect arranged accommodation in a safe motel. Different social workers visited daily. I was fortunate to be offered a unit in a DV refuge. I was grateful, but still terrified, sad and in a constant state of shock.

The kind people who worked at the refuge met me, and helped me with everything I needed – for months, till I was offered a suitable house. I relied on these strangers, who understood and could see where I was at – even though I had no idea.

While at the refuge I watched church programs of any denomination on television, and I wrote out anything positive to put up on a wall. I cried as I read them all every day, even when the wall was almost full. I said affirmations each day out of desperation, in my vulnerable, fragile state. Looking back, everything helped.

Although I was offered a house, I couldn't move in as I had nothing. The refuge staff arranged for a charity to help provide essentials. They transformed the house into an exquisite home using donated items, all set up by wonderful, hard-working volunteers.

Staff at the refuge arranged for me to see a doctor and a psychologist. I saw them long-term as I exhausted myself trying to run from the horrors that constantly consumed me. I lost all ability to function and a family member moved in to care for me. I started to let others help me as well.

I became terrified to go shopping. I would go late at night when it was closing, so I could avoid people. In my mind, I would think of the car park space that I was going to use. If it was already in use when I got there, I would go home and cry, knowing it might take days to get the courage to try again.

One night, when my car park space was vacant, I went into the shop feeling dead inside, without hope.

Someone walked towards me, and I tried to avoid them, walking past them. They came up to me and randomly gave me a bunch of flowers. I thanked them and walked around the store in shock. A small flicker of hope grew within.

I became creative about giving to friends or strangers, in many different ways. I was obsessive and excessive with this, trying to fill the void of brokenness deep within by blessing others.

Every day, I would write a list of things that needed to be done and I would try to do just one. Every morning I prayed and said positive affirmations or scriptures. I kept a diary where I could write or draw how I felt each day, so I could look back and see if I was improving, because my regular senses were numb.

I did DV group sessions with different organisations which supported me to heal and grow in a safe place.

I never thought I would ever be fully free or successful, or even laugh again. There was eventually light at the end of the dark, sometimes very long tunnel. I was thankful that I had genuine people and services who cared.

By attending one workshop or support group, I would find out more help that was available and I continued to heal and grow. I met fabulous women who also survived, who had compassion, and who understood that I was at times feeling fragile. It was great to build new friendships and important to find strength together.

I have learnt that life is precious, and I enjoy the simplest of things these days. I have suffered, endured, dreaded, and survived, and now I have a future that is free to be me. I choose to find my identity spiritually and I have relied on my faith for the strength to keep going.

My emotions and health have been pushed to extreme negative limits, which has come out in my appearance. I look in the mirror: I look tired, my hair has gone grey, and I see an aging, sad mouth – but I know myself better than ever. I feel beautiful in a humble way, because I know every line on my face, every shadow under my eyes and every grey hair is experience, strength, purpose. I am real and that is okay. My mouth may look sad now, but I believe that with every moment of joy and laughter, I am free to welcome my smile back.

I release negativity by writing messages on paper then burning them. I paint names or negative-feeling words on rocks, then throw them into the ocean. I love to dig my feet into the sand, watch the ocean waves pounding, breathe in the freshness and release any stress.

I'm free to be me! I will be growing more each day into who I was created to be. This has been possible because I have been reaching out to DV supports and medical services, joining groups to learn different strategies, meeting other women with similar stories, and keeping my faith in God.

I still have days that come at me with tormenting reminders;

they no longer take over my hope, faith or strength. I had to reach out for the light in my journey through the darkest tunnel.

Having freedom over my life means I choose what to wear and eat. I do what I like at any time and it's easier as I don't have to second-guess everything. I have been able to study, graduate, do many workshops and have many new experiences. I have a fresh desire to learn different things, have hobbies and try new exciting interests. My future goals mean I can enjoy my life to the full. Every decision is mine and I can save or spend money within my own reason.

Once I was out of DV and free to make my own choices, I travelled overseas and did many exhilarating activities that I had always secretly wanted to do. I have done a self-defence class, written poetry, bushwalked around mountains, visited exciting places, and improved my sleep patterns and self-care.

I am happy, with many new opportunities that I was blocked from having before. In my life, I am free to express how I feel joy. I can openly laugh, smile, feel and show confidence, have faith and spiritual beliefs. Sitting and reading a book is no longer a punishable crime because I am no longer a slave forced to continuously do hard work. I have learnt to trust again and balance life differently with the support of DV services and groups run by champion people, who are cheering on and celebrating survivors toward restorative healing.

THROUGH ONE OF THE GROUPS, I was asked to do a podcast interview for a sexual violence awareness campaign. I agreed, even though I had no idea what a podcast was. I was told that an email would be sent with information about the recording and the questions I may be asked, so I would know what to expect. I didn't read the email or questions in case I got anxious, triggered or freaked-out by having the time to think over it all.

This was my personal way of dealing with the process, to safely cope.

Every detailed care and support was in place for me when I arrived to do the podcast. I was calm and went in blindly, comfortable to answer my questions. The first question was something like, 'Who was significant to you, that you shared your experience of sexual violence with and believed you?'

I said, 'I have never told anyone about this till now.'

I realised in that moment I had taken a huge step, but I felt safe with the caring and genuine people with me in the recording studio. The interview continued in a casual, different direction after my first answer. I felt shocked that I had a voice that may help others. I recommended the great services available and told how their kind support helped me.

While I didn't have to describe violent sexual acts that had been terrorised upon me, I felt a huge relief in addressing – anonymously – what I had painfully kept hidden. I was strangely empowered and supported through the whole process and knew I had released this huge, dark, soul-destroying burden.

I can do anything, and I am finally free.

To me, he was the love of my life,
and my heart skipped a beat as he made me his wife.
I poured out my love till I was bone dry.
I desperately prayed to God, looking up to the sky.
I could see a storm coming, but I refused to take heed,
as this man was everything and all that I'd need.
That storm, then cyclone, then twister, hail and quake,
was reckless, violent, abusive and fake.
Once a strong woman who was whole, happy and fun,
I was purposely bruised, with no choice but to run.
Homeless and broken, never thought I'd be okay.

Angels came and carried me, and whispered that they'd
stay.
They said they could see me, and that I was now found.
They nurtured me till I could stand firmly on the ground.
They helped me build a life that's new
so I could see that dreams can come true.

FAITH GAVE ME THE STRENGTH TO KEEP GOING

I have relied on my faith for strength to keep going. These small steps of FAITH, accepting kindness, giving kindness, building trust, taking action and seeking help provided the light at the end of the dark and long tunnel. FAITH will set you free.

F—Flowers: Flowers represent accepting kindness from others and giving kindness to others. By accepting kindness, you will begin to trust again and restore your faith in the human race.

A—Affirmations: Watch church programs of any denomination on TV or YouTube and write out positive quotes and affirmations. Collect the affirmations in a book, journal or on sticky notes and put them up on the wall. Read out loud your affirmations daily, morning and night. Repeat each affirmation five to ten times. Be consistent, try not to miss any days. Affirmations help to change your mindset to being more optimistic and positive. They are the first step toward change.

I—Interests: Having hobbies or interests and doing activities that you enjoy can reduce anxiety and depression, improve overall mental health and wellbeing. Try activities you were not allowed to do during the abuse, or activities you loved to do when you were a child. Add in some new activities. To make it easier, attend activities with a supportive and caring friend or family member. Try writing poetry, walking in nature, visiting local places, painting, craft, taking a self-defence class or exercise classes. Try different self-care strategies.

T—To-do list: Write a to-do list every day of things that need to be done. Each day, try to ensure you do just one item on your list. Making a list of pressing tasks can help to reduce anxiety. Ticking off the to-do list helps you to feel like you are accomplishing tasks. As our mind forgets what tasks we have completed, the lists can remind you of how much you have achieved.

H—Help: Seek help from services such as Centrelink and DV Connect. If needed, go to a refuge. Make appointments with a doctor for referrals to visit a psychologist and/or a counsellor. Seek housing support and assistance with furnishing through services such as Rise Up. Attend workshops and support groups and learn different strategies of self-care. Healing and growth after abuse requires support from others and effort on your part.

For a downloadable PDF of the checklist above, go to <u>*brokentobrilliant.org/coercedtocourageous*</u>

CHAPTER 3
SURVIVING THE JIGSAW PUZZLE

'Coercive control is like a huge jigsaw puzzle with no box or boundaries. Others only see one or a few pieces (behaviours/incidents), unable to see the picture (pattern/intent). You are the only one who sees all the pieces, handed to you one by one to hold. It's a huge job to put the pieces together to see the whole picture.'

He hadn't spoken to me for two weeks now. Looked straight through me. Didn't touch me. Ate the dinner I had made with loud, aggressive scraping of his knife against the plate.

What had I done wrong? How could I fix it?

I couldn't stand it a minute longer. The tightness in my chest, the heavy dark silence throughout the house. I desperately needed to feel like I existed. Through the storm and heavy rain, I drove to a store. I spent as long as I could there, talking to the store person. The relief of that simple, friendly conversation – that I was not invisible. I absorbed that kindness and warmth inside me to help me get through another day.

I drove home. There was nowhere else to go.

The next night, we went to a dinner party. He parked his shiny black Mercedes in their drive. At their front door he became chatty, charming, gregarious, joking and affectionate, talking about me, but rarely to me. He brought them expensive wine, flowers and warm hugs.

Back in the Mercedes on the luxury leather seats, the silence started again.

A few days later, he woke up and started talking to me.

I had learned from previous times not to ask him about it. He would deny it, say I was being ridiculous, that I was tired or not coping or rant endlessly, angrily in my face.

I started to doubt whether the silence had happened. Had I exaggerated? But I was relieved that everything was okay and got on with my day.

There was no other way.

To an outsider, I had the perfect life: successful, charming husband, beautiful house, kids at an expensive private school.

Inside, I didn't recognise myself. My outgoing, independent, smart, confident and strong self long gone, now a shell of a person, whittled away, unnoticed and alone.

He wasn't always like that. At the beginning, he was attentive, with grand plans for us, making me feel so special and swept away.

After the wedding the first outbursts started, subtle at first but becoming more frequent and intense. Ranting, rages, standing over me, pinning me to a wall, cruel or indirect criticisms no matter what I did, shutting down my questions or requests with rants, 'accidently' breaking my treasured items, decreeing inconsistent rules for me to follow, isolating me from my friends and family through creating alternate plans or conflict with them, using personal information confided to him against me later. He would boast about his powerful contacts and connections, and wins over others who had crossed him.

There was never enough time or money for me or the kids' hobbies or needs, but unlimited time and money for his, with regular extravagant purchases. He controlled all finances and decisions. I did everything at home and for the kids; if I asked him to help out he would escalate and imply I wasn't coping, 'useless', 'stupid' and 'weak'. When there was an audience, he would fuss over the kids, a 'dedicated dad'. Before events he would start a fight, leaving me upset, and be charming when others arrived.

I didn't know how to respond without making it worse, and was speechless. I was so busy keeping him happy I didn't notice how long it had been since I'd seen my friends, and eventually lost touch. I seemed to apologise for everything. Without realising it, I was constantly tense, holding my breath, clenching jaw and body, trying to predict his mood. It was never safe to cry or show emotion, or ask for something I wanted.

Slowly my world became smaller, darker and lonelier, the shadows blocking the light more and more, but I just got on with my day.

And there were good times as well – as long as it was 100% his way. He would say how lucky I was to have him, that I would have nothing without him, that I should be more grateful for the life he provided me.

When he wasn't home, the kids and I would have fun together in the sunshine, adventuring, feeling safe.

I enjoyed my job, though he pressured me to quit, and I am grateful for how important this small defiance on my behalf would turn out to be.

FOLLOWING SEPARATION, he informed me that there was no place for me in the world or this life. That if I didn't do exactly as he said, he would take everything – the kids and money. Drag me through family court until I had nothing and was bankrupt, gut me, and leave me dead in a ditch. That I would never see my kids again. If I was to tell anyone anything about him or what he had done, contact the police or impact his status, he would hunt me down, destroy me and leave me for dead, making it look like an accident. That no-one would ever believe me.

He moved all assets and funds out of my and his name, including my savings in my bank account that he controlled. He demanded I leave the house and take nothing with me. I defied him again – I had nowhere to go.

I was paralysed with terror. It was escalating and evolving, dangerously and fast.

It took three people for me to realise this was not a normal marriage or separation. My manager asked if I was okay and told me to seek help. A professional tried to call a domestic violence (DV) helpline for me as she was worried about my safety. She couldn't get through, and I had to go home. After an incident, police referred me to a DV crisis centre, and a DV support worker visited me at my work. She showed me the power and control wheel and books by Lundy Bancroft. She asked me questions and I answered yes to all. It described my life perfectly.

It was like a fog lifted from my eyes and brain. I had not heard of coercive control before. There were no bruises – he had never hit me. I had never realised I was a victim of domestic violence.

I asked a lawyer for help, but he laughed and said, 'Until you show me a picture of you with a black eye it isn't domestic violence.'

The DV service provided significant short-term crisis support for which I was very grateful.

When police became involved, they noted extensive threats

and abuse including emotional/psychological, financial, property, technological, surveillance, isolation and more. They assessed significant risks and danger, and were very concerned.

They then spoke to him. He told them I had a mental illness, that I was unstable and not coping. They looked at his expensive house and belongings, believed him, and did nothing.

Serious safety incidents continued, with mixed responses. I stopped trying to ask for help. I managed it on my own.

As I well knew, any action on my part caused a dangerous reaction. After police involvement he escalated further, bringing in powerful reinforcements.

Family court commenced.

~

DEAR JUDGE/S

When I see fear on the face of my lawyers, too scared to or not permitted to speak up to you or the senior lawyers, I feel afraid and concerned.

When I am sitting alone on one end of the bench, with three senior lawyers on the other end and you towering above, cloaked in dark robes, within the windowless, soundproof, wood-panelled room, I feel intimidated, terrified, alone and small.

When you speak harshly and contemptuously to or about me, shout at me, rant, speak over the top of me, criticise me, and don't let me speak, while respectfully inviting senior lawyers to speak and ramble as long as they like, and I am required to stand silently and respectfully before you, I feel oppressed, shut down, silenced, disrespected and worthless.

When my carefully prepared, sealed legal documents – written by me through exhausting all-nighters while working full-time and caring for children and submitted on time – are removed from the court portal minutes before the hearing without notice or my knowledge, apparently due to a minor formatting issue, I feel vulnerable, helpless, invisible and powerless.

When you casually allow the senior lawyers to do an oral submission or submit unformatted documents on the spot with no evidence or rationale to the court, giving me only mere minutes to read, unable to respond before you make a decision with very serious safety implications and long term impacts for children, I feel helpless, devastated and futile.

When the rules of the court, including when consent is required and when it is not, appear to apply inconsistently and differently to each party, I feel powerless, defenceless and that I have no rights.

When you ignore/allow his constant non-compliance with court orders and processes, despite significant harm to children, delays, significant financial costs, and detrimental outcomes to me, I feel unheard, powerless, and as though I and the children are worthless.

When you do not read or consider the critical formal reports submitted by experts who raise clear risks to children, and you ignore their recommendations, leaving me no options to protect my children, I feel trapped against the wall, futile and devastated.

When you require constant court dates, hearings, thousands of documents, tens of thousands of pages, multiple reports, subpoenas, mediations, multiple expert witnesses, and many other processes over many years, I feel exhausted, overwhelmed and isolated with no time for family or friends, pressure on my job, broke and trapped.

When you flippantly comment on my financial devastation, poverty, the loss of my life savings and income, costs incurred so far, and indicate that this will likely increase to potential bankruptcy, I feel threatened, hopeless and scared about my inability to provide the basics for the kids and myself.

When there is no legal support, with legal aid denied, and community legal organisations telling me they can't assist or advise as my case/matters are too complex for them, I feel isolated, on my own, stupid and don't know what to do.

When you show respect, joviality and warmth to the senior lawyers, including lengthy chats about your social activities, conferences and long history together, and confirm that you have had private chats offline with them about this matter, I feel like you are emphasising their/his powerful connections, and I feel vulnerable, threatened and weak.

When I am forbidden to speak of the court process or my life to anyone, under threat of financial penalty or imprisonment, and unable to identify myself, I feel gagged, silenced, invisible and trapped in the shadows and secrecy.

When on the court/s journey, both represented and self-represented, I feel like I'm going back to the relationship, back to the past, to another world, outside of reality, where the outcome was determined just as he threatened at the beginning.

I am unable to leave the court/legal system or escalate concerns. I clench my jaw and hold my breath. It's not safe to show emotion or speak. I cannot 'leave', 'escape' or protect the children or our basic rights. This is my normal. I have nowhere else to go. There is no other way.

When you sigh loudly and rant at length about how irritating the case is to you and how busy you are, consider why this and other cases are dragging on so long, for so many years.

General domestic violence awareness in society is not enough. You alone have the power and discretion to either perpetuate or end coercive control, to hold individual perpetrators accountable, and for each survivor and each child to be able to escape domestic violence and end the generational cycle.

There is no other power, accountability or escalation point in this system or society. Responsibility for justice and change currently rests with each of you – in every decision you make.

Regards,

Victim

~

Dear Honourable Judge/s,

The short time I had with you gives me faith that a justice system could be possible.

Thank you for explaining the process clearly and respectfully to me as a self-representing person, inviting and allowing me to speak and respond uninterrupted, listening to me, clarifying, considering my words, spoken and submitted via the portal, and making a considered, measured and honourable decision. I felt respected, seen, heard and as though I am a human being.

Regards,

Survivor

~

To my children,

You are brave, strong, smart and kind. I had wished for you a joyful, carefree and safe childhood with boundless potential and future. Build your self, freedom, confidence, opportunities and happiness, and find a good normal. I love you always.

Mum

~

To other Survivors,

The abuse evolved post-separation. It was systemic and ongoing, and utilised the children. I developed and adapted my survival, defence and rebuilding strategies during different stages and times.

These are my suggestions to you.

Seek support: Access any available DV or related support services. Crisis and long-term support are both critical. I am forever grateful for my long-term DV support person who taught me to put down my heavy armour when I can, to give my poor body and mind a rest, and only wear it when I have to. She was beside me on the long, dark journey, holding her lantern, navigating through the dark maze.

Connect: Find other survivors and survivor underground networks, online and in person. Day or night, you can reach out to someone who understands and try to help each other with the legal system. To feel heard and validated; it isn't absurd to them like it can seem to others. Our stories and the abuse tactics were so similar that we joked that we all must have married the same man. Laughing at situations in a morbid way helped release some of their power and the tension.

Socialise: From having no-one, I built many friendships through online groups and meeting people with common interests, building new skills and lasting connections. Do activities that bring you joy.

Set boundaries: Choose who to trust and confide in. Some colleagues/friends have been supportive, for a chat and assistance in different ways. I will never forget the shame I felt when an executive commented at a DV event that they couldn't understand how an intelligent woman could get caught up in that. Learn to say no if you can't take something on, and respect your available energy and time.

Learn: Understand how perpetrators work, their tactics, and strategies to deal with them. There are many helpful books and online resources. Learn from other survivors.

Respond: Don't react, be measured and calm with schools, professionals etc. Limit interaction with the perpetrator. Vent the emotion/reaction with a safe person or in a safe place. Get someone to read your drafts to take the emotion out. Respond to the essentials only.

Manage security: Check technology, devices, accounts and email addresses are secure. Potentially replace or change them. Inform organisations to protect your privacy.

Manage finances: It is possible to live on very little for a long time – op shops, giveaways, second-hand everything. Be resourceful and reframe it as an adventure.

Manage court: Be organised, use a good file structure, keep copies of everything, have templates of common court documents, document everything. Take a McKenzie friend[1] to court, learn property and parenting processes, learn system and court rules to ensure all the process is aboveboard. Raise the rule/law/issue at the time if required – be calm, respectful, and speak confidently. Maintain a 'court bubble', and don't overinvest your time, money and energy – it's a black hole.

Manage setbacks: Feel, grieve, get back up, one day at a time, keep trying, harness anger to mobilise action constructively, think laterally, consider options, be patient, drive action, evolve, find alternate ways or contacts.

Connect, soothe, release, recover: Use meditation, grounding exercises, breathing, music, exercise, humour, nature.

Protect health: Look after your health, for you and your children. The exhaustion and constant stress can impact your long-term health significantly. Become aware of and listen to what your body is telling you, and care for it.

Be kind: Being offered a small kindness, a word or gesture, can seem surprising and foreign but makes such a difference and keeps you going. Be kind to yourself, and others. Know you did the best you could in the circumstances.

Make a safe space: Create and grow your safe spaces, compartmentalise them from the shadows. Work can provide stability and normality, and help rebuild self-confidence. Do what works for you.

Advocate: Drive change for those coming behind you. Take every opportunity and step out of your comfort zone. Be brave and bold.

From a Fellow Warrior.

LIFE IS different now in many ways. A recent interview question surprised me. 'What hobbies and interests do you have?' Years ago, I couldn't have answered it; I wasn't allowed to have a life. But now there is so much to say. The day before, I had been paddling tranquilly through the trees, with the sun glinting on the water and my skin, and a kind, steady hand helped me ashore.

A warm, balmy evening around the crackling glow of a campfire, our tent nestled into the circle of our friends' tents. With chatter and laughter, the adults relaxed after a happy, carefree day of swimming, rafting down the creek and exploring the bush. The kids ran around the campground playing spotlight with torches, making a happy ruckus. We eagerly planned our future adventures. Leaning back in my camp chair, I gazed at the stars, breathed deeply and felt the sensation of peace and freedom wash over me.

In the beautiful old wooden hall, warm lights chasing away shadows, I could feel the rhythm of the music. Every part of my body connected with my mind and breath as I spun across the dance floor gracefully, amid the other dancers, fully present in the moment and melody. I felt the warm, safe touch of my partner, with innate unspoken communication and trust as we moved together, connected and equal, creating a moment of exhilaration.

HE IS STILL THERE, in the shadows, ruthless and relentless. But I choose to treasure and focus on the moments of light, peace and happiness that would not have been possible before. I have created a safe place with kind people, sunshine, colour and fresh air for myself and others, and especially for my children to come to when they can escape the dark and the shadows. They will always have somewhere to go.

LIFE HACKS FOR REBUILDING YOUR LIFE

LIFE HACKS are the strategies for surviving post-separation abuse and the legal system, and rebuilding your life.

The LIFE HACKS in my letter to survivors are strategies you can use to diminish the impact of the dark and the shadows and move toward light, peace and happiness. Create a safe place with kind people so you can live your life.

L—Live and laugh: Create fun and joyful moments and memories to build balance and hope. Find your people and your communities to feel connection and belonging. Laugh to release the tension and reduce anxiety.

I—Inform yourself: Inform yourself to know what you are dealing with and to help you face and fight the fear that arises from the unknown. Inform organisations about your situation to help protect your privacy and keep you safe.

F—Find yourself: Rebuild your sense of self. Discover your talents, likes and preferences. Identify your goals and make a plan. Celebrate your achievements and strengths. Nurture and respect yourself.

E—Emphasise health: Look after your physical and mental health. Become aware of and listen to what your body is telling you, and care for it. Make time for essential health checks. Sleep, meditate, learn grounding exercises such as breathing exercises, use music, exercise, humour, and walk in nature. These actions will help to regulate your responses, help soothe, release and process ongoing trauma and abuse, and aid recovery.

H—Hold records: Establish processes to keep you organised for court. Create a good file structure, keep copies of everything, have templates of common court documents, and document everything. Get a printer and scanner. This will save you time and stress when you need the information.

A—Advocate: Speak or act to help and support others on an individual level and advocate for constructive change at a system level. Being an advocate gives you back your voice, a way to be heard, and provides hope and a path forward. Advocacy helps to drive change to the system for those coming behind you, to help survivors transition to thriving.

C—Calm: Respond in a calm and considered manner, rather than reacting, especially in dealings with the system/s. Vent and release in a private and safe space. Pick your battles as it's not possible to do it all.

K—Kindness: Kindness is being helpful, generous, considerate, and caring, and holding space. Be kind to yourself and others. Accept kindness from others. Being kind and accepting kindness can help you to get through difficult days and to heal. Kindness can reduce feelings of stress and improve wellbeing.

S—Support and Sharing: Access any available domestic violence or related support services, formal and informal. Share your stories with other survivors to give and receive practical and emotional support and learn from each other, and feel less alone. Have a safe space where you can talk openly about your experiences without judgement. Acknowledgment and validation may not change the situation but help healing.

The patterns and warning signs of coercive control are becoming well documented, along with its significant impact and far-reaching damage. When the legal and other systems are required to put the pieces together and see the whole picture, the puzzle of coercive control can be addressed, held to account and solved.

For a downloadable PDF of the checklist above, go to brokentobrilliant.org/coercedtocourageous

CHAPTER 4
MY GIFT OF FREEDOM AND LOVE

'I've found the courage to stand up for myself after being downtrodden for so long. I learnt that the past does not define your future. You can achieve your goals and enjoy a better life.'

I wasn't sure I even liked him, particularly on our first 'date' at the drive-in. I spilt my drink in the car. I said, 'I'm sorry.'

He berated me for being careless. 'I will have to spend all weekend cleaning my car now.'

The more I saw of him, the more uncomfortable I felt. He was pressuring me to marry him. He was rushing me into the next phase of the whirlwind, but there was nothing special or deep in it for me. My gut said no.

I had joined the military forces at 18. I had grown up in a domestic violence situation and I couldn't wait to leave home. Now, I only had 16 months to finish my enlistment and he was deploying for 12 months' active duty. I thought it would be a good compromise to wait until those commitments were completed, but he said no.

He ingratiated himself into my family. Mum liked him and so did my little brothers. He had a Jekyll-and-Hyde persona, but people never saw it until it was too late.

Two years into my military service, I received a letter from my mother. She had without notice or consultation organised the wedding. I was getting married two months later. I had to discharge on my twentieth Birthday and come home. (In those days, if you were under 21 one of your parents had to give permission for military service.) I was horrified. No explanation, no answer!

I had to pay fifty percent of all the costs as my contribution to the wedding, and buy the dress and veil. I ended up broke, sad, and dependent. My life changed significantly from a soldier to a coerced bride, to a wife who, 49 days later, was introduced to domestic violence.

Everyone got what they wanted, except me.

~

WE MOVED INTO AN OLD-STYLE HOUSE, partitioned to create a small flat with a view out to the sea. The rent was cheap at $15 per week, which suited him. The elderly property owner was disturbed by his angry outbursts and our arguing. She said, 'I have never had tenants like you before.'

I quickly found a position in the city for a large company. At Christmas, all the staff were requested to give a gift for the children's orphanage. He wouldn't allow me to buy a present. So, on payday I bought a doll, wrapped it and placed the gift under the tree with all the other gifts.

The staff Christmas party was only drinks and nibbles, and it was embarrassing when he rocked up uninvited, unexpected and angry.

'You are coming home now.' He grabbed my arm firmly and

marched me out to the car. He was enraged and his driving was frantic. Arriving home, he pulled me out of the car and roughly pulled me into the flat and punched my left arm black and blue from elbow to shoulder.

When we arrived at his family home to visit, his mother saw the bruising and asked, 'What's that bruising from?'

I said, 'Ask your son. He can tell you what he did.'

He just sat there and didn't say anything.

Her reply was, 'Oh that's not nice, don't hit her again.'

Like that was going to fix the situation?

HE DEPLOYED OVERSEAS, and I did everything 'right', sending food parcels and writing letters. He came home on leave. We had five good days together and it was a pleasant experience. (I thought he might have reformed.)

The 12 months of his deployment passed all too fast, and he was coming home. His letters had changed, and I was worried just thinking about his return.

Our first child had been born while he was away. I drove with Mum and the baby for the trip to the airport.

I did not know which airline he was coming on. Of course, I went to the wrong terminal and had to race to the other. I saw his angry, contorted face coming down the escalator. I knew that look.

He didn't even say hello or look at our eight-month-old baby. All I got was, 'Where's the keys?'

'Here,' I said, as I quickly took them from my handbag.

We walked in silence to the car. He took off, driving on the wrong side of the road. I reminded him, 'You are in Australia now – get in the proper lane.'

You could have cut the air with a knife for the long drive

home. No-one spoke. I really wanted to see my Nanna that afternoon, but Mum said quietly, 'Wait until tomorrow.' My Nanna was my best friend and she died peacefully in her sleep that night. I felt bereft and abandoned.

~

WE WERE USED to the peripatetic nature of military service life, with posting changes and packing up and moving elsewhere. His next posting was for us as a family, but I didn't think I'd be safe living abroad with him, so I told him he could go by himself or ask for an Australian posting, which he did.

After settling into the house, I was visited by a male welfare officer. Apparently, I was not being a good wife and my husband had made a complaint as to his welfare and needs, and I needed to support him. I needed to change my attitudes. It was all about him. Apparently, he had painted me as a lazy wife.

To him, I was a chattel that he owned. He would check my purse at breakfast and come home at lunchtime to see if I had gone out or spent money. The house had to be spotless, all day, every day. I ironed his uniforms and polished his shoes. There were lots of arguments, slaps, pushes and loud, angry arguments. He was even jealous of my time with our baby.

It was all my fault; I got the blame and the abuse.

I made friends with a couple of other military service wives and their husbands. We decided to do a three-day fishing trip on a houseboat. My son was now 16 months old and I was five months pregnant. By Day 2, he was getting jealous. Everyone was talking and playing cards, but he was sulking. He would not join in.

Later in the afternoon, he called me onto the deck and started to berate me. Then, his hands were around my throat and I could not breathe. I struggled, trying to fight him off. All I could think was: what happens if he kills me? Then the two other men jumped in to rescue me. Thank God for my life.

Sadly for me, we were not friends after that.

ON THE MOVE AGAIN, with two children and another on the way. The military service house was cold and condemned. Grass grew up between the wall and the floor. No hot water. A gas stove I hated. For washing clothes, a copper boiler that would literally burn your eyebrows if you got too close.

He bought a kero heater and put some carpet down. Sometimes, he filled the kerosene can because he always had the car but, other times, I had a long walk to fill it – with two children in the pram.

Then he chose to move into the single men's accommodation in the city with 'the guys', where he could enjoy freedom, partying, and meeting women. He lost his second or third wedding ring in that move to the city.

I did not care; it was peaceful for us. I also had a great neighbour next door, and that was such a bonus.

He did come home on the weekends for a quick visit and that was always good for an argument.

Physically, I was glad he wasn't around. Emotionally and psychologically, it was less stress. Financially… that was never going to change.

WITHOUT WARNING or discussion with me, he took his discharge from the military service. Just like that, it happened. He bought a house for us, in his name only of course, and we moved into a home with a secure yard for the children to play.

I hadn't asked his permission to get a job, but I needed my own vehicle. So, I applied for a waitress job in a restaurant and started working two or three nights a week. I really enjoyed the few hours I worked outside the house.

One of the regular patrons was a wine merchant and a good customer. He brought with him some half-sized bottles of wine to gift to the staff.

I left my bottle on the kitchen table so he could see it the next morning. He said, 'What did you do to deserve that, exactly?' The insinuation of impropriety was clear.

'We all got one,' I said. 'It's no big deal.'

He made some very derogatory comments about me, and it was on for young and old and quickly escalating.

He went into the bedroom. I followed him down the hall because I knew what he wanted. He was trying to get the twenty-two rifle out of the wardrobe. He was pulling the wardrobe door open, and I was pushing it back, with the baby in my arms. I was really scared of how far he might go.

I screamed out to my five-year-old son, 'Quickly, get the little kids out of the house. Run! Get outside!'

Timing and miracles are everything. My sister's car turned into the drive just as the kids ran out of the house. I heard my son screaming, scared, and crying out, 'Daddy's going to kill Mummy!'

She grabbed the kids and put them in the car. My brother-in-law rushed in and got him out of the house. All I could do was breathe and feel thankful to God for my life. The gun was removed.

THERE WERE other occasions that turned nasty. Too many. I was a physical and nervous wreck.

He should have stayed in the military service. After trying different jobs that didn't suit him, he decided to join the navy. I got excited at the thought of him sailing the ocean wide for months on end. He did all the applications and the interviews, ready to join up, and at the last moment, he reneged.

Instead, he dragged us thousands of miles for a new job, away from the few family members I had. Our house had to be sold, and we were on the move again. Changing schools and kindy, leaving friends. I didn't want to go. In two weeks, he left, and we followed about six weeks later.

We were starting all over again. The proceeds from the sale of the house was all spent on boys' toys. He flipped $20 at me and said, 'Get yourself something.'

Within three years our family had totally disintegrated.

I CAN'T REMEMBER what I did this time to make him angry, but he grabbed me around the throat and banged me against the wall and that was the last straw. I had reached the end of my tether.

I said, 'I'm leaving you. I just can't do this anymore.'

He reminded me, 'You're just a chattel I own, and the kids are millstones around my neck.'

I had no plan. I was winging it. I had four children. I owned nothing and had no money.

I knew I was the better person to look after my children, but he sabotaged, manipulated and indoctrinated the kids against me because he owned everyone. His parents bought him the best solicitor in town, while I had no representation in court. The judge didn't acknowledge me at all. He won custody of three and I had the youngest child. He didn't want them; he just didn't want me to have them.

I was stuck until I went back to work. Payday could not come quickly enough. I leased a flat in the industrial area – one bedroom with a bus stop at the door. I was 'allowed' a couple of basics from the house. We had our clothes and little else.

The three older children came over every second weekend.

That's when the kids told me about 'Daddy's sleepovers' at home with other ladies. He had no morals.

Then, the stalking, spying, and break-ins to my flat began. He would snoop in cupboards and drawers and move things around. As soon as we got home, we locked the door and hung bells on it, to keep us aware and alert.

THIS WAS BACK when everything was done by snail mail. There were no emails, websites, mobile phones, podcasts or Google in those days. It was a matter of 'letting your fingers do the walking' with a phone book in one hand, change in your purse, standing in a phone booth hoping to find out where you could access help for yourself and then apply.

I applied to Social Services for the single parent's pension and to the Housing Commission for a roof over our heads and cheaper rent. I was grateful for both these services as I had no family support at all.

Our new home was quite liveable – two bedrooms, a bathroom, lounge and kitchen, and a small balcony at the rear. It was a bit dowdy, so a couple of friends volunteered to buy the supplies and together we gave it a fresh lick of paint. It looked a lot brighter.

I was given a double bed and a single for my daughter. We had a coffee table, a record player and two records, no television, no phone and no car – but we were safe. The basics of a roof over our head, beds to sleep in, and food (often only rice) to eat, as we sat on the floor around the coffee table, made us luckier than millions of others.

I HAD NEVER HEARD about red flags. I lived in the era when wife bashing and assaults were called 'domestic disputes'. Very few police attended DV calls and the culprits were rarely if ever charged.

I tried to lodge an AVO, but it was not accepted, not entered and never actioned.

I didn't know anything about domestic abuse counselling services back then, either. I just tried to find my feet and move forward. I loved my children and as a mum, that was my role. We were all scarred from those years of abuse. All I wanted in my future was to live well and help my children be the best in life that they could be and take back what the enemy had stolen from us.

FREEDOM! No more assaults. No more being scared to open the door. I learnt that sometimes you go through tough times, because the black dog bites, but life is for living.

I drew up a list of pros and cons. A friend told me you need a one-year plan to start with, then a five-year plan. My plan wasn't stuck in concrete, it was fluid. Just as well! You must think about what you really want in a career and then work out how to achieve that goal.

I worked hard to rebuild my life after abuse and also had to deal with a society that frowned upon me as a single mother. I worked for two years in a religious school but lost my job when the new principal discovered I was divorced.

I did not give up. Fortunately I had social housing and a good friend who could mind my daughter. I took many jobs and developed an eclectic resume. Some of my jobs were enjoyable, some were part-time, some were awful. If I didn't like it, I just looked for something else.

With two other mothers I scored some work on a building site. We dropped our kids off at school, went to work, and left in time to pick up the children. They were hot 35-degree days with 100% humidity. The money came in just before Christmas.

Through my resilience and ability to learn quickly I worked in everything from government positions to setting up my own business in beauty therapies. I tried sales and turned over one million dollars in a month. I tutored. I became a celebrant.

I started dating someone I had known as a friend. At first, I didn't want to marry again, but I loved being spoilt and taken care of. Eventually, we did marry. He was the love of my life and a great husband and dad who accepted my children as his own. I became the breadwinner after he suffered an injury and was never able to work again.

I worked long hours to keep everything going, including caring for my husband and elderly mother. It was hard, keeping all the balls in the air.

Then I really did retire, choosing to look after my husband. My heart broke the day he died.

I GREW into a strong and determined person, knowing I had the ability and the confidence to get those good jobs and make decent money.

Give everything a go and take every opportunity that comes along. It fulfils your life and builds your self-esteem. I learnt that the past does not define your future. You can achieve your goals and enjoy a better life.

It's a new day and a new life and I am so grateful to be free. I was handed a new way of living for myself and my family. I am set free from the shackles that held me fast in despondency for so long.

I don't know that I am courageous – I never really thought of courage applying to me – but I am free of the burden of living a lie and putting on a face for the sake of peace, and that is a relief.

There will always be good and bad days, but the bad is manageable when you are in your own head space. I'm not saying that every day is a sweet day, but when you look back on what a sad day used to look like you realise you are closer to the rainbow than the darkness.

Be happy. Spoil yourself, because you have more than earned the right to live free and enjoy every day to the best of your ability.

Dear friends,

So many things have changed in my life. I am me, the person I used to be in those halcyon days of the military forces and the fun we had. Life is just getting better and better. I shared with you all on many occasions when I felt down and broken. I thank you for your support. Only steadfast friends stay the course.

I have regained my confidence and moved forward, and I am having a divorce party. I wish you weren't so far away but I know you will toast me with some bubbles. The divorce is far more exciting than living in a nightmare marriage.

Freedom and equality is the most favourable way of life, and I am happy. I am managing my life and rebuilding relationships. I've found the courage to stand up for myself after being down-trodden for so long. I am hoping to visit as many of you as I can, or meet up at our next reunion, when I have saved some money and you will see how I have flourished and that I am back to being cheerful and happy. Life is to be lived and I just know the world is my oyster.

Sending love.

MY GIFT OF FREEDOM AND LOVE

Timing and miracles are everything. I had courage that I did not know I had. I took opportunities and learned many skills. My GIFT of freedom and love came through setting goals, recognising my inner strength, building friendships and taking opportunities. Through these GIFTs I was able to receive the greatest gifts of all:  freedom and love. You too can build a better life and enjoy the GIFTs of happiness, freedom, and love.

G—Goals: A good friend advised me to create my goals and plans. I created a one-year plan and then a five-year plan. I kept these plans fluid so I could take up opportunities that arose. Setting goals and planning helps you to move forward in life. A goal and a plan help you to prioritise and focus on what you want and value.

I—Inner strength: I did not realise how strong I was. I struggled, went through stress and kept going. I was strong. Recognise your inner strength. You have lived through anguish and fear. You have sought support and are looking at rebuilding your life. This is inner strength. Keep going. It takes inner strength to take on the struggles you face every day. Be kind to yourself, take one step at a time, acknowledge your strength and courage to break free, and move forward with your life.

F—Friends and Freedom: Through the ups and downs of life you will find your steadfast friends who stay by your side during both the good and bad times. During the downs, unfortunately, some friends will show their true colours. You have the freedom to choose who your friends are. Friends helped me paint my house, looked after my children, and one friend became the love of my life. Open your heart to your friends. Connect, laugh, work, and support each other. Good friendships provide help, support, kindness and care. They keep you grounded and real.

T—Take the opportunity: Miracles and timing happen in life. Take up the opportunity to try a new job. To move house, to meet new friends. To enjoy every day. Do what feels right for you. Not every opportunity will be right. It can be scary to try something new, to step outside your comfort zone. Outside your comfort zone is where you learn and grow. At first, take little opportunity-steps until you feel more confident. Then trust your gut instincts and take other opportunities as you and your confidence grow.

For a downloadable PDF of the checklist above, go to brokentobril liant.org/coercedtocourageous

CHAPTER 5

SURFACING INTO
THE SUNLIGHT

'I love my new voice. I am my own best friend. When I look at my reflection in any mirror, I see a kind and loving human sprinkled with warrior dust.'

Authentically, I bare my soul for you, unravelling my once-secret life, opening wide to these desolated times. My truth. Will you see me? Will you reconsider or confirm your views of coercive control? Will we feel something real together? I am prepared to take the risk. Are you?

I FOUND myself and my small children once again in a women's domestic violence refuge… numb. Drenched in his sour sweat as my fears of failure swept over me once again, I cried alone in the maroon darkness.

I had decided I'd actually go out for New Year's Eve with my good buddies. My mum had offered to take the kids for the night and encouraged me to go out and have some fun. Usually, I'd stay home with my adorable kids and we'd watch movies together while my husband partied. I was the dutiful wife, or at least I tried to be.

That night, I really danced. My body rocked on as I lost myself on the dance floor, saturated by those heavy bass beats. The lyrics of my favourite songs hummed and infiltrated my soul. Ahh! My happy place, there you are!

I arrived home late, blissed out. I glided like a zephyr of joy into our marital bed. He grabbed me hard. His salty breath trickled onto the back of my neck. As Mr Green Eyes erupted, a wild beast raped me that night. I ran to the other bedroom and slammed the door shut. He followed me and smashed me, his fists to my skull. My rose-coloured bubble fell, ruptured, flattening me into nothingness.

I was pretty blurry, but I do recall feelings of shock. I felt numb, invisible, and could hardly string two words together. But secretly I blamed myself, over and over again. If only I had just stayed home like I usually did, this wouldn't have happened to me.

A few days later, I turned up to the local court in our regional town. My abuser was never charged for sexually assaulting me and a protection order was never mentioned. The magistrate told us we needed to get some marriage counselling.

My heavy feet shuffled listlessly from court that day, hearing the overwhelming voice in my head: 'No-one there thinks much of me, so why should I care about me either?'

In the years leading up to that New Year's Eve, in the end he didn't even have to speak. I could sense his mood by the way he walked, how he slightly tilted his head to the side and the shape of his pupils. I became a great observer, trying to predict the simmering monster within him.

Before he arrived home from work, I would madly rush around and try to make the house look tidy. I knew I'd cop it somehow – if it looked like the children and I had played, if the washing was piled high, if the dishes weren't done, if dinner's aroma wasn't echoing in the air.

His ute would splatter through the rusty back gate. I'd hear the clanging and the rattle of his tools and ladders, and panic, wondering what I had done wrong today, what adjectives he would use to describe me today: hopeless mother, fat, lazy, useless. He'd bark at me, 'I wouldn't look at you if you were crossing the street twice, you've really let yourself go. You should have had dinner ready by now. What the f___ have you been doing all day?'

I frantically tried to juggle all the expectations imposed on me, with little kids in tow and a baby to feed. I'd serve his dinner as he snarled at me like that old blue cattle dog across the street. He'd say, 'What's this slop?' and push his plate away in total disgust. Every year he bought me a new cookbook for my birthday or Mother's Day and yes, every year I didn't bother reading it. That little bit of rebellion still flickered inside of me. 'F___ you,' I said under my breath.

While I unpacked the plastic bags from our local supermarket, he'd grab the receipt and trace his finger through it. Saying ever so sarcastically, 'How much did this all cost? There is nothing to show for this in the fridge or the cupboards to actually eat. You can't do anything right.'

My two greatest loves were my kids and my dog. My dog was a rescue. She snuggled with me and listened when I cried into my pillow at night. Mr Green Eyes would walk past her and give her a shove or a push, or yell, 'Get out of my way, you mongrel thing,' then laugh to himself in a very odd way that sent chills along my heightened vertebrae. My dog strongly despised him and, like mine, the hairs on her neck prickled as he walked by.

I had no access to the joint bank account. He made all the

financial decisions and other major decisions. Mr Green Eyes would often say to me that I couldn't be trusted to manage the money – this was his role as the head of the family. My job was to stay home, cook the meals, clean the house and look after the children.

He demanded I stop taking the children to weekly sports training and weekend sport matches. His orders to me: 'You need to be at home, not gallivanting all around the countryside.'

He made it difficult for me to work towards any financial independence and sabotaged my dreams to finish university or maintain my work and part-time jobs. He would often not show up to care for the children when I was rostered to work on the weekends.

Sometimes I'd just had enough…

I'd pack up the kids and some clothes and we would just leave. We went straight to the local domestic violence refuge. Stay a while, lick my wounds, then feel better – but I always went back to him. He would be so remorseful and tell me he had changed. Become a present father to our children and read them stories at bedtime. This never lasted. We danced on this dysfunctional merry-go-round for many years.

The women's refuge knew me and my children well, as we were frequent flyers. They patched us up, gave us a safe space to recover in. We could breathe again. I participated eagerly in the women's support groups. I found talking with and meeting other women going through similar things helped me. I realised for the first time I wasn't alone.

Our circle of love and hate continued for more than fifteen years, and our kids felt the intensity of our instability in the ebbs and flows of hysteria which was our home. I felt ashamed.

I thought I just needed to try harder and try to keep the peace. Yep, I thought, I'm not enmeshed in that domestic violence wagon wheel of dysfunctional relationships.

My love for him was intense. I so desperately tried to ignore, deflect, pretend or just blank that sh__ out.

I saw my patterns of self-soothing with food and my poor body image spiralling out of control. Anything to numb myself from the realities of my life as I subsided into the abyss. He would belittle me constantly in front of our children.

He told me that I wasn't allowed to use birth control. He said that he didn't want any more kids, but it was my responsibility to use the Billings Ovulation Method. This caused me a lot of stress, so I decided to have my tubes tied. He strongly opposed my decision, refused to take me to the hospital, refused to visit me and refused to pick me up after my surgery.

I CAN TELL you the exact circumstances of my light-bulb moment. I was sitting at the in-laws' kitchen table. My father-in-law was yelling, saying horrible things to his wife, as he often did. I glanced across at my mother-in-law. She was such a kind, caring and beautiful woman. I thought, 'Why would someone treat her so badly? She is such an angel.'

I knew in this precise moment – suddenly clear as a bell. My eyes saw for the first time. I saw a live clip of my own future in my head. I was frozen in time and space. I was going to be in my sixties living this way and this would be my life too. If I continued to stay in this kaleidoscope of pure crap that was my marriage.

Very soon after my epiphany, I started planning my escape. I was pretty good at leaving by now. I packed our knapsacks with clothes, filled our little van with petrol, the dog, my kids, and my most treasured processions, and drove out of that town.

I never even looked back once at my beautiful home in the rear-vision mirror as I let our security go.

THE FRIENDS I thought were my friends soon disappeared, or betrayed me, or some even blamed me for the violence.

Some stayed. My true friends listened to me for hours as I cried, got mad, yelled and made many poor decisions.

My recovery had begun.

My grandmother had been thrown through a wall by my grandfather. My mother had copped two black eyes and betrayal from my own father. My grandmother and my mother left. My father in turn rejected me, despite my attempts to reconnect with him as an adult. These strong women gave me the strength of a lion, and hope.

They listened and offered me and my kids emotional support, for which I am forever grateful. My kids and I were marinated in their unconditional love.

I never felt judged by those who supported me. My network of strong and wise women helped me, while I unravelled and grew in my own time. They gave me space to work out my own solutions and supported my decisions. My mum never said to me, 'I told you so,' not once.

We relocated. I found another domestic violence women's support group and then, much later on, fortunately found my soul-level recovery in the Broken to Brilliant tribe. Feeling connected to others like me helped me to feel part of an authentic sisterhood. These connections gave me many insightful tools for my ever-evolving recovery and growth.

As I unpacked my baggage, I started to heal. Finally, I had found a safe space to express my story without judgement.

I went back to university and worked two part-time jobs and cared for my children. We ended up homeless, twice. I fought for affordable housing and, after many years, we finally found some stability.

I tried to stay afloat. I felt I was failing my children. I had mountains of mummy guilt for the times that my kids spent in before and after school care, vacation care and childcare.

I sought help from my GP when I was feeling overwhelmed and anxious, and when I thought I might get really depressed. When I started having flashbacks and nightmares, I was referred by my GP to a psychologist. I started taking antidepressants which really helped too. I found a psychologist that I felt comfortable to share with and I worked on healing my past trauma. I floated in the ocean and walked in the bush and played under waterfalls. I learnt new constructive ways to help me move forward in a positive direction. Forward is forward.

In the midst of my early recovery, I was diagnosed with ADHD, an eating disorder and a hearing impairment. The missing puzzles were starting to connect. I had often been overwhelmed by feeling as though multiple TVs were broadcasting on different channels in my own head. With treatment, these were reduced to one channel. The noise became blissfully white. No wonder school had always been so darn challenging for me. I had just always thought I was dumb. My teachers and my father said I'd never amount to anything, and my husband also undermined my intelligence, so eventually I believed them.

We were living in a densely populated Department of Housing suburb next to a very busy train station. Most days, I struggled to feed my children and to keep a roof over our heads, or to have enough fuel to drive to university lectures or my jobs, or transport my kids to and from school. The electricity and phone bills and car rego were always overdue. There were the trips to pawnbrokers and the numerous student loans to keep the wolf from the door.

But we were safe, we had peace, and I was determined.

I WAS angry and bitter for a long time. I could almost taste the flames of my fury.

Over time, I discovered that the most powerful element of my own healing was forgiveness: for those who had harmed me, for those who had never believed me, for the systems that had tainted us as the undeserving poor.

When I was able to put into action authentic forgiveness, it actually set me free. As I forgave others, I in turn forgave myself. This mindset released my concealed anger, rage, nightmares, helplessness and fear. I filled up that empty hole in my own heart and transitioned to fully loving me again. Things became easier and easier. Believe me, I'm still a work in progress. We all are, aren't we?

Strength came to me slowly, but I kept taking one step at a time. Simple things like getting out of bed were tough some days when every essence screamed to stay under the blankets and hide from the world. Moving at my own pace was more than enough for me.

I know within the core of my being, no-one has the power to change me except me; this is my job. I am the mirror for my children to see. I knew they were learning from me. What I did, how I chose to live my life and how I treated others. I chose to no longer be a victim but to be a survivor.

I was determined not to fail my children. I set my sights firmly on that 'cap and gown' – to graduate university. I was motivated to be a positive role model to my children. I knew my children were watching me.

I now acknowledge I didn't have great role models as a kid, so this wobbled my compass for a while. It doesn't mean you can't set a new course. We found our new village. I found my people in Domestic and Family Violence women's support groups, my children's school, play groups, my workplaces, parenting workshops and my local neighbourhood centre.

I couldn't have done it without my support network and these amazing humans I am honoured to call my friends and family. They all helped me raise my kids to bloom into self-assured adults.

I graduated from university with a Bachelor degree and then postgraduate qualifications. I found out I wasn't dumb after all. I now work in a field I love, and I have provided financially for my children who are now following their own dreams.

I can now buy enough food every week to feed myself and my family. I can pay the electricity and phone bills on time and buy food. I am able to meet the day-to-day running costs of my home.

I was able to buy my very first home and my first brand-new car. I was able to take my children and myself on holidays. I relish making my own financial decisions and I'm actually a great budgeter.

I love my new voice. I am my own best friend. When I look at my reflection in any mirror, I see a kind and loving human sprinkled with warrior dust. Gone is the timid and insecure person that used to stare back at me.

A wise woman once told me, 'Every night when I lay my head on my pillow, I say out loud that I am so grateful for a roof over my head, food in my belly and the love living in my heart.'

I know in my core I am free, I am kind, and I am still learning.

My adult children are my walking, breathing proof that there is recovery and healing after abuse. I hear it in their music and when they laugh. I see them parent their own children with kindness and connection. Surviving abuse and domestic violence brings a kind of genetic wisdom and empathy that you just can't quite put into words.

In our survival, we fostered a family culture of empathy, truth and fighting fair. This bond we have built is unbreakable. Our life without abuse and coercive control has become a landscape of freedom, where fear no longer defines me or my children.

SURFACE AS A SURVIVOR

You too can SURFACE from the depths of coercive control and abuse, free to be your own best friend. You can recover and heal. Try these steps so you too can move forward to a life of compassion, empathy, honesty, friendships and a family life free of fear and full of laughter and love.

S—Support: Seek support from trusted friends and family. Work with a doctor, counsellor, psychologist or psychotherapist you feel comfortable with, to help you address the impact of abuse. Seek out women's support groups, programs and services to find your tribe, a place of acceptance and knowing.

U—Understanding: Stop, step back and learn about abuse, coercive control and its impact. Developing insight and understanding about abuse and your inability to change the person who is using abuse is another step in the healing journey.

R—Role model: Be a positive role model for yourself, other survivors and your children. Foster a family culture of empathy, truth and fighting fair. Be a good budgeter so you too can move toward owning your own car and home, and go on holidays.

F—Forgive: If you are holding a grudge, feeling knotted up and angry, feeling vengeful, and are focused on the past abusive acts, forgiveness could be a tool to help you. You could forgive the person who harmed you, forgive yourself for the mistakes you made during the abuse, or both.

Dr Swatz[1] says forgiveness 'is an active process in which you make a conscious decision to let go of negative feelings whether the person deserves it or not.' To forgive as part of your healing journey is your choice. It does not mean you condone the past wrongs.[2,3] Forgiving helps to give you the psychological 'space' to be able to love and care for those important to you.[4]

To forgive is a process and you need to be ready for this step. Recognise the impact their abuse had on you and your children. Work through the grieving process for the loss that you have experienced. Accept that you cannot control another's behaviour. Work with a counsellor or psychotherapist to assist the process. You can use forgiveness affirmations or write a forgiveness letter and reframe that forgiveness to be beneficial. Be inspired to forgive watching YouTube videos. Forgiving can set you free.

A—Appreciation and Affirmations: Practise the art of appreciation daily. Make a mental list of the things you appreciate or are grateful for and say these before going to sleep and upon waking. Pick the little simple things to get started, for example: 'I am grateful to be reading this book.'

Work to silence your inner negative voice. When you hear these negative words, you can use an affirmation. Say to yourself, 'Stop,' or, 'Thank you for sharing.' Then immediately have your inner voice say something positive about you. I am strong. I am brave. I am…. Hit repeat. Keep repeating your positive affirmation until the inner voice becomes less prominent.

C—Courage: You have taken the first courageous step toward recognising your own value by leaving the abusive relationship. You have heard so many negative words about yourself it will take time and courage to counter that message. Journalling about what you value and what you love doing can help you see yourself in all your amazing strength and courage.

E—Education: Classes, courses, education, TAFE qualifications or university degrees are all steps that tell you that you are worth it. You are not all those words you were told. It gives you a place to belong. A place to focus on something different. To learn new and interesting topics. Meet new people. See the world in a different light.

For a downloadable PDF of the checklist above, go to brokentobrilliant.org/coercedtocourageous

CHAPTER 6
SISTER, SISTER

'Today was different. Today I was done. Today, I decided on me. … I am taking me back.'

*S*hhhhhh! *Sister! I got you. Wake up. You gotta live, sister.*

I heard you, like a drop into infinity. There you were. Have always been.

Like a shotgun to the head, I'm awake, and coldly aware of his steel hands around my neck. Just as he has done many times before. Steel hands around my neck.

But this is the catalyst that topples. I hear you, back to the beginning, and will myself to open my eyes.

Live, breathe, sister.

I'm on my back. Skin ice cold, air so thick and hot. The sickly-sweet smelling room is where I am now.

When I was first put to work on the street – for my own good, he said, pimped out – why not? I was good at it. To pay my way, that's what he said. That was constantly beaten into my head.

All I was good for. Because whatever other money came in went on drugs, alcohol, repeat. Like a washing machine on quick cycle.

Had it really got to this?

How did I get here? Well, anywhere else would be better than waking up in this hellhole, hey?

Most nightmares end there, but mine? I lived it. Stink oozed from my pores like a hangover that never really ended. This is what he made me. What his love looked like. How much he loved me, he said. Jeez, it hurt. His love. It hurt.

I gave in to it. It was easier, till it wasn't. An abyss.

~

Light bulbs, arrows were starting to turn on, as if the electrics didn't work. I was achingly feeling every emotion all at once. But not really feeling at all. Definitely not happy. Happy? What's that? What I was doing wasn't actually living. A zombie. A watered-down version of who I used to be. It wasn't me staring back with naked eyes. Essentially, I wasn't home.

A 'woman's lot' smile plastered on my face. Rehearsed excuses ready to go. Oh, I'm just a klutz, accident prone, didn't have my glasses on.

I left a thousand times, ran out the door, gone. Gone every day to survive. Somehow, I removed myself. Just floated up and disappeared. Like watching a bad movie. Not the fairy tale I'd been led to believe. I zoned out. I didn't consciously know that at the time, though I would come to learn it. Like many other hard lessons, too little, too late.

~

So, you escape within yourself. They don't know, couldn't know, it's the only way to survive. Every day you walk, breathe, move. But it's not you. Not anymore. Not for a long time. As if a passenger on a bad Elvis tour. You know you should have jumped off the bus. You want to get off, but you can't. You can't stop the scratched record playing over and over.

No, it's loud.

Yes. Nothing but a hound dog.

I wasn't lucky. My prayers didn't get answered. My requested help just didn't come.

I was left for dead. Even to this day I can't fully recollect what I went through. But there was no mistake. I was left for dead.

HE WAS RAISED SHARP, but he couldn't account for every variable. He couldn't watch me and have his thumb on me twenty-four-seven.

Somebody saw me. Though a drowned rat, I was seen. Screams do get heard.

As if the red seas parted! There is a God. As if He himself came through and opened the gates and shone a light on me. In that brief, bittersweet moment I was asked: Are you okay? Do you need help? How long has this been going on?

Is that concern, kindness, compassion?

Such lies he drilled into my head. I heard this far-away voice: I'm not sick, I'm okay. The rehearsed excuses again.

Coming out of the haze, I felt a hot cup in my hand, a blanket wrapped around me. I was absolutely soaked through, throbbing, head raggedy, breathing in my own mist.

Only then did I start to tally up the pros and cons. What else had escaped me? What else didn't I see? What else?

A ghost of myself. Took me eons. The pain of all that absolute trauma.

Suffering had left its dirty, unforgiving marks on me. Like stupid jailhouse tattoos you got at 17 years old because you were told they were cool. What a joke. Then you covered them up with lotus flowers, years later, when you should have known better. As if the flowers could hide the trademark tattoo of his name across your heart. As if you have dementia.

You ask yourself, what did I do wrong? I must have deserved this. It can't be real. It's just too horrific to comprehend.

Such a spell he put on me.

But not today. Today was different. Today I was done. Today, I decided on me.

Sister. Sister.

Sister, sister. I hear you, like the sweetest song on a summer breeze. Sister.

I am taking me back.

CHAPTER 7
THE SLOW-BOILED
FROG ESCAPES

'I remember my former self. I wanted to be her again – confident, independent, energetic, and social. But I am better than her. Once broken, made whole again through my determination … repaired with gold and more beautiful for it.'

Coming around while lying deathly still, my newborn baby is gently placed on my chest. I feel the elation of motherhood. The powerful realisation that I am responsible for another little life who is completely vulnerable.

Before I can hug him, things change.

Tiredness creeps over me. Blood pools internally and my eyelids grow heavy until I no longer have the strength to open them. My limbs cannot move. I am unable to speak.

I hear everything with impeccable clarity. The emergency response team is notified. Being slid to the trolley is excruciatingly painful. I am there in body but my consciousness floats above. I am calm and detached, knowing this is a defining moment of my life… or death. The air feels freezing against my cheeks. My life experiences flash through my mind. I am plunged into darkness with a bright light emanating in the distance.

I feel reassured when I hear his familiar voice through the urgency around me.

The doctor advises, 'Her blood pressure is dangerously low. There is no blood for the heart to pump, a blood transfusion is necessary. Your consent is required.'

My relief vanishes, replaced with absolute terror, confusion, and shock as he says, 'Blood transfusions are not permitted for JWs.'

Why would he tell such a lie? I have never been a Jehovah's Witness! I am vulnerable like our baby, powerless, without any ability to respond. I want to shout, 'THIS IS NOT TRUE!'

The person I love, trust and have built a family with is prepared to discard me. To let me suffer or die, without so much as a kind touch on my hand. I am without hope, absolutely betrayed.

Thankfully, just before I am taken into the operating theatre, my sister arrives to visit. The doctor asks for her direction. She indicates I can have ANY and ALL measures that will sustain my life.

I lose this memory to my subconscious for years, too painful to consider.

~

WE FIRST MET when he interviewed me for a job. I sat opposite him, nervously. Panel members solemnly scrawling. His eyes locked onto mine, smiling. He nodded agreement to my considered answers, encouragingly. When escorting me from the room with quaint chivalry he whispered, 'You nailed it.'

Our work brought us together again and, despite my reluctance, he pursued me with intoxicating persistence. He was in a long-term relationship; I was in a dead-end marriage. A whirlwind romance ignited, fed by romantic gestures, spontaneous generosity, and long, emotionally intelligent conversations until early in the morning. He indulged me and appreciated all the time we spent together, sensing what I was needing and starved of.

'You are the love of my life, my soul mate, we are meant to be together,' he whispered repeatedly.

Love blossomed. The honeymoon phase was a long and euphoric high. I was on a pedestal, swept into the delusion we could make this work. He encouraged me to leave my marriage, promising support.

How he said we would manage household routines sounded reasonable and desirable. A relationship of equals with a realistic work-life balance. The opposite of my marriage. I was hooked on the dream, the imagined paradise, the enviable couple living a charmed life.

He was publicly charming and charismatic. I felt special that he wanted to know me completely and took interest in everything I did. I bathed in his intense love and attention. He showered me with compliments on my sense of adventure and lust for life, my living without regret. He lamented the time lost and experiences denied him due to his previous (fictitious) life of religious service and leadership. Although his regret saddened me, I looked forward to a full and meaningful life together and eventually getting remarried as he proposed.

I was intrigued that his apartment was impeccably clean. This made sense, given his previous employment in the food industry, an industry renowned for fastidious neatness. He still held skeleton keys from one position, and volunteered as a Justice of the Peace, an upstanding member of the community. His other work roles had included positions of great responsibility and trust, so I felt my young daughter would be safe with him.

His home was also completely devoid of creativity. There were no photos, books, art, or personal effects; he explained he had left his marriage with nothing. A blank slate.

HIS CONTROLLING WAYS crept into our relationship like cancer. All horizontal surfaces were clear and wiped daily, the bedspread perfectly flat and pillows positioned just so. He intentionally damaged my sentimental items because he wanted to dust easily. He took control of tasks because he wanted me to need him, to see and appreciate his value – and he wanted to undermine my independence.

There was no defining moment, but a gradual, insidious change from feeling symbiotic to more like a prison, with endless, increasingly dehumanising tests over a decade.

Public sex, swinging, forever demanding more frequent sex, and ensuring I felt responsible for his gratification or else he would go elsewhere. When I was unable to provide what he wanted he felt justified to use a prostitute. He wanted other men to desire me and envy him for his 'trophy' partner; then he punished me for their attention. He wanted me to act provocatively and dressed me scantily in size-ten clothes, then accused me of embarrassing him with my appearance and behaviour.

There were tests of the extent to which I would help his friends and family, to see if I was 'enough'. Endless acting. Arduous, expectation-laden trips overseas. I had to do more and more to please him.

I starved myself to look as he wanted, wore my hair long and down. No matter what I did, he complained he was 'missing out,' getting a second-rate relationship when he deserved the best. I was inadequate, somehow cheating him of the life he felt he deserved.

Catching up with my friends or family was challenging. He would judge them as if they were not worthy of my time or his. He put others down to build himself up. I hoped that with time and love his self-esteem would improve. His privacy, public image and reputation were tantamount, while mine were used for his purposes. He could embarrass me, publicly shame me, or share private information or photos and ridicule me like a child.

When I discovered his affairs, his proposed method to restore my trust included full phone access and responding to calls and messages immediately. His ulterior motive: to have full access to my information in return for his 'transparency'. At his insistence, I slept naked for his convenience. I lived in self-defence mode, avoiding conflict, jealousy, and unpredictable emotional turmoil.

Life was death, by a thousand cuts. Exhausting avoidance with cat-like sprints over broken glass.

I no longer made social arrangements, fearing the repercussions. My plans were always insufficient anyway. I reduced my participation in conversations as offering an opinion was risky. He recycled conflicts we had resolved. He controlled and devalued, and used a plethora of false accusations generated from his fears and guilt. I never knew if his reactions would be loving and supportive or condescending. He commanded the pulpit in our lives, talking excessively to control the narrative. Sharing only enough to make me believe that I knew him or that there was truth in his dialogue.

I overthought everything he said and dwelt on his subtle hints, his suggestions laden with veiled threats – while he dismissed flirtations with other women in my presence. I was confused and isolated, an emotional wreck. He changed the narrative so often there was no sense of reality, no direction without him. My belief in myself was white-anted, eaten away, leaving a deceptively delicate shell.

If there were no drama, he would create it. He had to find 'the edge' that elicited a response until I was left screaming, 'Leave me alone!' over and over. The numbness of alcohol sustained me. I felt ashamed of my position, weak. Disillusioned by his perpetual deceit and affairs. I could no longer trust anyone, let alone myself. More than anything I lamented about what was the right course of action for our children. He was capable of being wonderful when he wanted, so I made allowances in hope.

I did not want to give up, fearful through social conditioning that the failure would reflect negatively on me. He harnessed my fears, manipulating me further with each of his affairs with empty promises if I could only forgive him again.

I was deceiving myself. I had sold my soul to the devil.

HOMEWORK HURRIEDLY COMPLETED before he returns home. Chopping vegetables for dinner while arguing, again. I look down at my hands and notice the blood. I have sliced a finger again while defending myself from his opportunistic manipulation. Shark-like attacks where I defend myself from his false and ridiculous accusations, where escape is difficult.

'STOP FIGHTING!' the kids scream. He will never let go. He can smell the blood before the injury and be lurking and lapping – he has to have my reaction. The kids want to be peacemakers but have to retreat. I feel belittled, disconnected, and dissatisfied but there remains in me a willingness to accommodate.

If I only did this or did not do that...

HE COULD SWITCH it on whenever he wanted and then tear me to shreds the next moment. Blocking my exit and working on devaluing me – my weight, intelligence, communication, supposed infidelity, my relationships, my deepest fears and insecurities… anything. His attacks would surface on any occasion, any little moments when one could ordinarily recharge: toileting, showering, breastfeeding, travelling. He was determined I would have no downtime physically or emotionally.

I could not be lonely; I was never alone.

I FOUND myself sitting in my car yet again, the rain rolling down the windows, condensation concealing my despair. It was late. I was cold and desperately isolated. I was unable to think of what to do, the pervasive brain fog hindering my ability to make sense of my situation or make even the simplest of decisions.

Who would understand and believe me? Who could comprehend the truth of my experiences with the covert narcissist who had taken over my life? I was feeling like a hostage, a willing victim who had compromised my values and beliefs, my very existence and being.

My fat, ugly tears fell. Thoughts swirled between how to survive if I stayed and how to escape. Where could I go? What more was I willing to give up, to compromise, for the sake of this unhealthy relationship? Primarily, I felt regret for my poor choice of a father for my children. I felt alone and empty without him and hopeless with him. In every way I was defeated, defused, and disabled. He had ultimate power and control. I did not know when or how it had happened.

I DARED to call out his controlling behaviour and emotional abuse only once. His response was swift, and my doubts re-emerged. I had never seen him so angry; he was usually so calm and in control. Perhaps his greatest fear was that I was discovering his true nature: the wolf in sheep's clothing. He demanded a retraction. I was 'crazy' and abusive for wrongfully accusing him.

I fought back once. He fell back in surprise as I pushed him away from me after another verbal onslaught. From then on, I was painted as a woman with 'anger issues' who had 'physically assaulted' him.

He was convincing. He could easily manipulate people and say what they needed to hear. Institutions, schools, friends, neighbours, legal professionals… he could manipulate everyone to believe him about anything he wanted, to elicit sympathy, gain control, obtain victim status, maintain his innocence, and always control the dialogue.

His power to manipulate others was intimidating. I recognised he would be a formidable enemy; he terrified me.

ALL THE WHILE, I was getting infections, and sex was painful. He would blame me, insisting I did not love him and was making excuses. In a way, it was true. It was impossible for me to connect intimately with someone I could not trust. He insisted I look at him during sex while I cried in physical and emotional pain. It felt like rape. I switched off, willing it to end.

His romantic relationships were a trail of destruction, ex-partners' 'failings' conveniently used for sympathy to entrap his next victim while he was actually the cause of their suffering. I was simply the next casualty. He lured his compassionate targets like a spider, trapping and sucking the lifeblood out of them. Recycling love letters because he was incapable of authentic love. With flexible morals and ethics, and endless sex and searching.

I AM at work on autopilot, with a happy front and a myriad of secrets. Today, I have mandatory training in Family and Domestic Violence.

I sit watching the case studies and listen with uncontrolled tears streaming down my face. Every case study is my story –

without physical abuse. Is my experience domestic violence? I am not crazy, I need help. How have I gotten to this point? I no longer recognise myself.

The realisation hits me hard. Finally, I hear the whisper in my gut that tells me I need an escape plan. I have to say, 'No more!' to end this suffering because he will continue to use me for his convenience.

I FELT ELATED to have reached the decision to leave, the latest affair being the final straw. I reached the point of knowing that I had been that slow-boiled frog. It was time to give up hoping for something better from this oxygen thief.

His empty words to bribe and placate fell on deaf ears. I left, moved to my safe house, got a new job, and set my goal to extract him from my life as quickly as possible. The surge of relief and sense of freedom was amazing and frightening.

Once I realised how crazy it was to lament something that had never existed, it was easier to get over it. I was grieving a relationship that never was and never would be. There had been nothing but empty promises and lies.

This abusive relationship I had endured for a decade had shaped me – there is no immunity, even for the most resilient.

I remembered my former self. I wanted to be her again, the one before meeting this alien: confident, independent, energetic, and social.

But I am better than her. Once broken and made whole again through my determination. I reflected on the Japanese term Kintsukuroi – broken pottery repaired with gold and made more beautiful for it. This alien has not beaten me.

I read extensively, listened to podcasts, and attended support groups. I invested in myself and loved my healing journey.

My workplace arranged professional counselling and trusted

colleagues supported me during work hours when I struggled to hold it together. I stayed in touch with my truest and most loyal friends who have sustained me. We have long conversations about my experiences that were formally taboo. They listen, supplying sound judgement to my irrational fears and feelings.

Professional support and education was vital due to my persistent brain fog. It was so difficult to explain to others when it made so little sense to me. My emotional turmoil was all-consuming, filling sleepless nights with anxiety, fear, and premonitions that he would act on his threat that I would disappear, never to be located. I had no idea what he might have been capable of or how far he would go. I knew he had the means and knowledge to fulfil this threat, as he had done for all too many other threats.

My family were my primary support, standing with me without judgement. They helped emotionally and practically, allowing me time to heal. Their unconditional love buoyed me through the solitary months of COVID-19 isolation.

It took my sister to make me realise… he never had my best interests at heart.

SECONDARY BETRAYAL by mutual friends was a hardship I had not expected. I was ostracised, amid broad disbelief that what I said had been happening could be true. Suggestions that he was 'just going through a bad time', when I had been the one in the private hell.

He refused to recognise my boundaries, flirted with me and threatened me in my own home. Stupidly, I had believed his vow that we could be friends for the kids' sakes, and he would help maintain my home. He bargained to the very end.

I visited the police station more times than I can remember. Each time, I took weeks to develop the courage to seek help.

Eventually, I was fortunate to meet with a specially trained officer who supported me to apply for a temporary protection order.

I experienced further self-doubt when the patriarchal hierarchy decreed my experiences were not domestic violence – I was 'vindictive'. I felt like I was playing a game of chess; he was always three moves ahead and I did not know the rules.

Now I have my passion and zest for life back, embracing every day with a new purpose because I can see the beauty in my peaceful existence. I can be authentic to myself, knowing my worth. I can have the downtime I need to recharge without guilt. I exercise every day, pursue interests and hobbies and invest time in creative pursuits to draw, paint and write.

I accept my history and I have a greater understanding of the need to have boundaries, love, and trust in my relationships at home. Having my freedom is the greatest gift. I had to reclaim my liberty from this alien as he would not return it to me graciously.

I can be a dag and wear my pyjamas all day if I want to and leave my wet towel on the floor. I can do everything I need to run my household and have a successful career and happy children. My house is a safe place, a HOME, with ornaments, photos, art, creativity, mess, pets and such fun, joy, and laughter.

Standing in the shade with tired, aching muscles from working in my garden, I have lost track of time again. I am planting under the lilly pillies, feeling so alive! Filthy hands rest on my hips as I stretch my back. I take a deep breath in, eyes closed, and feel such contentment. The blooming flowers above delight my sense of smell. The busy bees all around are collecting nectar in a loud frenzy, creating their consistent loud hum which transports me to another dimension.

Another deep breath of sweet air and I become acutely aware of all my senses. My face and cheeks feel radiant, a smile creeps up at the corners of my lips. Years of tension falls away and troubles slide off me.

The bees disturb tiny petals above in their pursuit of nectar, showering me, soft as snowflakes. My skin is brushed clean. I feel so alive, healthy, and free.

Freedom made better by having endured the incarceration of my soul by a coercive, controlling partner. He will deny it, minimise it or control the narrative.

But this is my truth.

BECOMING WISE

I became WISE to his manipulation and control tactics after attending a workplace domestic and family violence education session. I trusted my gut instincts, sought support, and finally escaped. I now have passion and a zest for life. You too can be WISE, alive, healthy, and free.

W—Workplace family and domestic violence sessions: Attend sessions on domestic and family violence in the workplace or community. These sessions will help you to understand that what you have been told is your fault is not your fault. The anger, the games, the crazy-making, the put-downs – this is abuse. By attending a session, you will know if you can access leave from work, counselling and a range of other supports.

I—Instincts: Instincts are those gut feelings, the butterflies, the body tingles. You instinctively know. Research has shown that in complex situations your brain can unconsciously process a large amount of information and provide you with the answer – for example, when you intuitively know that someone is lying. It is wise to listen to your instincts, especially if there is a short time frame. At other times, don't dismiss your instincts, but think about your response and seek professional support to help you with a plan to escape, to keep you safe and to support you on the journey of recovery and rebuilding.

S—Support: Support will help make this journey a little easier to navigate and work through. Some people have family, friends or work colleagues who can help. There is also professional support from trauma and domestic and family violence informed counsellors, psychologists, psychotherapists and psychiatrists. Police and professional domestic and family violence support workers can provide extra support. Seek help from services that know about domestic and family violence for support and referrals. Seek support to help you on your journey.

E—Escape. Exercise. Experience each moment: Don't go back. Seek help to develop your escape plan. When you escape, breathe, and experience the little moments in life. Focus your attention on the present moment. The sun warming your cheeks. Your children giggling. By taking the time to experience each joyful moment you will reduce your stress and anxiety and improve your overall happiness. Experiencing the moment will recharge your body and soul, giving you the fuel to continue on your journey. Each day, add exercise to your routine – a daily walk, some digging in the garden, free exercise programs in the community. Exercising can improve your mood, make you feel better about yourself, reduce stress and improve wellbeing.

For a downloadable PDF of the checklist above, go to brokentobril liant.org/coercedtocourageous

CHAPTER 8
STUDY: YOUR STEPPING STONE TO BEING YOU

'Education was my golden ticket… I sought out courses for personal growth and self-improvement. A qualification was the major stepping stone toward me creating my new career pathway and lifestyle.'

No. I am *not* dumb or stupid! That was the first thing I learnt about myself after escaping my second bout of domestic violence (DV) in my thirties.

I had escaped one abusive relationship at 21 only to fall into another web of coercive control and unbelievable acts of manipulation. Every unpredictable moment of every day, my nervous system was on edge.

It was education that finally stopped the cycle, thanks to a psychologist who challenged me to believe a single mother from a trauma background *could* go to university.

~

At 17, I entered my first intimate partner DV relationship, the darkest nightmare of my life. Shameful secrets live deep within my muscle memory. I am still unable to speak, think, recall or write about this time without feeling nauseous or faint. He was an animal. I was coerced into his trap and remained his hostage until I escaped four years later.

This wasn't an adult relationship. That would have had elements of loving equality, reciprocity, autonomy and independence. This was different. This was immature, childish, highly emotional and volatile, based on jealousy and possession. I was an object to him, not a person with feelings.

Following the trauma I received from this man, a gynaecologist at the women's hospital told me that I would never be able to have children. Fortunately, my future would reveal that my body did heal, and I had the great blessing of giving birth to children later to another man. However, I spent many very painful years of my life grieving the loss of ever becoming a mother.

From the beginning, I was ensnared by his violent control; it was overt, obvious, tangible and extreme. I simply did not know how to get away. Daily, I was being psychologically conditioned to become completely powerless. My friends and family were afraid of him. His own family were afraid of him. No-one offered to help me for fear of retribution.

Even *I* can't work out how I let this happen. *Why didn't I just leave?*

Being on the receiving end of frequent intense violent acts created a fragmentation in my brain. Memories of this time were shattered, scattered, and splintered – like my body. My mind blocked out many traumatic events to survive, yet disease now resides in my body to let me know that the memories are still there, deep within my cells.

When I was 15, I made the innocent mistake of being emotionally and physically intimate with this guy. It was a school-holiday fling – 'puppy love'. It ended when the holidays did, for me. But it seems our brief connection turned into a lifelong pathological obsession for him.

The first red flag: one wet weeknight he showed up randomly at our home, hundreds of miles from where he lived. That was weird, but we let him in, patched up his grazed arm from a skateboard accident and sent him on his way. Later, he showed up on our family holiday and, somehow, we let him stay with us. He showed up many times in many strange situations, always needing rescuing like a lost puppy. I should never have been so kind to him, but that was in my nature, so he manipulated it.

He was diagnosed with terminal cancer at 18 and had hugely disfiguring surgery. I felt enormous compassion for him, but this kind emotion soon saw me trapped within two threads of control – one from my mother, who coerced me to gift myself to a dying young man; and secondly from the domination and violence that were unleashed when I moved in with him.

His cancer took over our lives. I began making allowances for his intense behaviours – the physical and verbal aggressions, the pathological jealousy and the dark, dark moods.

I felt ashamed and deeply embarrassed. So, I became more isolated from my social networks and, unknown to me, he had driven everyone away with threats of violent harm if they dared intervene or support me.

I was imprisoned within a torturous environment, one that no-one would ever believe; one that made me doubt myself, my mind, my reality; filled with unspeakable acts. The perpetrator relied on the silence of the abused.

To counterbalance the darkness of my private life, I worked hard to pretend everything was normal to the outside world, that I was okay, that I was happy. After all, I felt *I* had created this mess. So, I felt responsible to fix this or live with it. My mother reminded me that I deserved everything I got, that I made my bed, *so lie in it.* So, like a good girl, I put my mask on.

In my newfound madness, I even paid off my own expensive engagement ring to show the world that he really was okay, that we were okay. That would have been the biggest red flag of all though, because I raised that one myself.

Every day was 100 hours long.

Being very young, our money was always tight. He never had a problem with me working and using my money to live on as he dipped in and out of work. His employment uncertainty fuelled his inherent anger, so I walked on eggshells every moment, never knowing when he would explode without boundaries – in supermarkets and carparks, at gatherings of friends, at home, at work.

Physically, the abuse was constant – a punch, a shove, a kick, a burn, a push. This would escalate to choking, often. It could be day or night – always sober, drug-free, and unpredictable. He would only attack areas beneath my clothing lines, so people at work could never see what was happening to me physically, and he controlled what I wore to ensure nothing was ever seen. This included ripping up my clothing if he thought it made me look too attractive.

He learnt these strategies from his war veteran father who beat his mother constantly. His father also tortured him and his brothers in a shell-shocked haze; there was no professional support for returned soldiers. I witnessed similar violent dissociated behaviours being acted out within my own family of unsupported returned soldiers.

Emotionally, my intense fear eventually became numbness, dissociation and alienation. I can't recall feeling love or kindness, there was no fun, no joy. I only recall his anger, hostility, moodiness, jealousy, bitterness and hatred.

A familiar emotional pattern, similar to my father's. Psychologically, I had been belted and melted into losing all concept of myself. As a child I was a people pleaser, for my own survival and so that we could be a 'normal' happy family.

WITHIN THIS RELATIONSHIP, I became merely a question mark.

There was constant berating: *useless, stupid, barren, slut, whore, idiot, ugly, fat, dumb.* Accompanied by the throwing of plates, glasses, tools – whatever was nearby or in his hand. *You can't cook, this is disgusting, you're useless, you're f__ing him aren't you, can't you do anything right, this is filthy, what do you do all day, lazy bitch, you're frigid, you're so fat…*

As in psychological warfare, my mind absorbed all these layers of incorrect beliefs. His commentary was graphic, filthy and disgusting, his actions perverse. He would lock me in our bedroom, tear up my clothes, create elaborate traps using fish-hooks and blades so I couldn't escape from our home.

The rent was exorbitantly high, so at one point he began to arrange for me to become a drug mule through his bikie connections. He had access to firearms. He was deadly-serious and cruel. Like other Stockholm Syndrome victims, I adjusted to this heinous situation. I behaved. I complied to survive.

And I did.

IT TOOK years to get away.

I became totally isolated. There were no refuges in remote towns to escape violence in the late 1970s. There was nowhere to turn for professional support. With no internet, no mobile phones, no counsellors back then – only church-run groups to turn to if women needed help – the male-dominated mining towns hid silenced women, who kept their heads down and hid their bruises to keep a roof over their children's heads.

There was certainly no possible way for me to have an adult conversation with this man about our relationship, ever. To sensibly discuss 'we should end it', or 'we need to separate' was just not an option – in case you are wondering why I didn't just grab my bag and leave.

But I know that if you are reading this and you are in a similar situation, you do get it! Read on, as I will give you some hope.

The violence kept escalating and I felt the end of my life was imminent. I was consumed by creating a survival plan. *How on earth will I get away?* My family were thousands of miles from me. I needed to get to them to get help, even if they were his allies. But I had to go to them *with him* as he would never let me go anywhere without him, except to work.

Sickening as it sounds, I thought if I planned to marry him – a reason that would give me the chance to be alone with my family – I could make my move. One desperate Sunday, I suggested this.

We started marriage classes. My mother, who loved the fact her daughter was sacrificing her life for the happiness of a dying cancer victim, planned an occasion. A cathedral no less.

He punched me constantly as we drove… the entire trip. I still recall pain upon pain. His knuckles were large, his muscles bulked. Like everything he did, I had no idea why. There was never any rationale behind his behaviour. Just pure cruelty.

FINALLY, I am alone with my parents, just days before our wedding. I tell them *this cannot happen*. That *he's going to kill me*. I show them my bruises.

My father's attitude on this occasion is kind and understanding. He says *of course, we must cancel*.

My mother screams *it must go ahead*. All of her friends will be there and she would be embarrassed to call it off. Besides, *you can leave him much easier if you are married to him. You cannot leave him standing at the altar, or he will kill you!*

ONE VERY BAD NIGHT, a few months after the wedding, he threw me around our apartment like a rag doll. He pushed me to the floor, kicked me with his steel-capped boots, then grabbed me by the shoulders and pinned me up against the brick wall. My head cracked. He began choking me, hard. Spitting foul words at me. His hands got tighter and tighter around my neck.

I didn't know what I had done, I never knew what I had done. I was just cleaning up after making his dinner.

He was sober, he was always stone-cold sober, he never took drugs. But he was insane and pathologically jealous, full of anger and hatred.

He decided to drag me outside and pushed me into his car. I was limping and terrified as I didn't know what he was going to do. I thought: *tonight I am going to die.* As we drove up the crest of a hill, a police car came toward us. I was going to jump out of our moving car and scream for their help. Then I recoiled – it was dark, if they drove past and didn't see me, he would kill me for sure.

He continued to drive in silence, and we arrived at the local hotel.

He dragged me up the stairs into the public bar. Men sat facing the bar smoking and drinking. He pushed me towards the bar and spat, *Hey, who wants to f__k her?* I looked to the ground. Ashamed. Alone. Afraid. He pushed me toward them once more. *Go on, she's all yours… who wants to f__k her?*

The room became silent. They turned to look at me… then at him… then gradually turned their backs on us and continued to talk. No-one helped.

See—he shoved me toward the exit—*nobody wants ya, ya barren whore.* Outside, he punched me and pushed me into the car, then drove me home and raped me.

I survived another night.

I had to get out, alive.

MY GREATEST MOMENT of vivid self-realisation was the night the police finally came.

A work colleague who had witnessed DV as a child had helped me leave him at last. Seeing the way he interacted with me in a restaurant one day, Jenny whispered, 'He hits you, doesn't he?' I looked downwards, ashamed. She said quietly and firmly, 'Grab your bag, walk with me to the toilets. I am getting you out of here.'

We walked out through the other side of the toilets, grabbed a taxi, and I never went back.

Jenny found shared accommodation for me through our workplace. I was no longer isolated and had somewhere safe to live.

He spent weeks driving the streets with a shotgun, to find me. After two attempted abductions he broke into my shared accommodation and seriously assaulted me.

Later, two uniformed police officers stood over me. One said, 'No man has the right to hit any woman, ever. No matter what she has done.' Long silence. 'It is *never* okay to hit a woman.'

I will never forget this empowering moment. This was the first male in my life to ever tell me this. I was the child of a violent alcoholic father, and the granddaughter of violent men who physically, sexually, financially and emotionally abused my grandmothers. I took in this new information and held it very close to my heart.

LIVING in group housing with protective work colleagues meant I flourished now that my perpetrator had gone, as per police orders.

I immediately filed for divorce and ceased all communications with him. I was never alone going to and from work, or at home. Gradually, I joined sports groups and kept myself busy, working full-time and playing softball, netball, squash, darts, dancing.

Soon, however, I began to drink like a fish. To avoid the pain of remembering. So I wouldn't have to wake in a pool of sweat unable to breathe with those hands tightly around my throat – unable to tell if this moment was real, or a nightmare.

I didn't know it back then, but I was suffering terribly with post-traumatic stress disorder (PTSD). Hypervigilance, depression, nightmares, anxiety, insomnia, palpitations, and nausea were just part of the huge array of my everyday physical and mental health symptoms.

I eventually formed a new relationship, but it also turned out to be abusive. Sudden violent outbursts; continual lies; gaslighting; manipulation; criticism and put downs; controlling and isolating behaviours; financial domination; excessive drinking; multiple infidelities and staying out all night.

My second husband blocked me from receiving medical treatment in the regional hospital for my postnatal depression, as prescribed by my doctor. I would find out years later, this was because he was having an affair with a nurse – one who worked on the ward I would have been admitted to.

On reflection, I question the diagnosis of postnatal depression, as that diagnosis blamed *me* biologically. I was a victim of domestic violence and I strongly suspect my symptoms actually resulted from the abusive environment I was living in – something that was never investigated in my medical assessment.

With the support of a girlfriend, I boarded a plane in a haze of suicidal postnatal depression and mind-numbing medications. After ten long, hard years, I had left my second husband. It didn't feel like it at the time, but I guess I had guts and determination – not for myself, but for my children. I would fight fiercely to protect them from harm and do anything to give them a safer life.

Education was my golden ticket.

After leaving my second disastrous relationship I needed and wanted to take personal responsibility for my life. I sought courses for personal growth and self-improvement. I wanted to understand myself, people, their motives, their behaviours. I needed to work out who I was, who my family were, why people do what they do, and why I am who I am.

I had the good fortune to have a few sessions with a psychologist with lived experience of DV. She asked why I hadn't been to university. I'd left school during Year 11 and thought this major goal was inconceivable as a single mum in her thirties. No-one in our family had ever gone to uni – it was way out of our league.

She guided me to sit the STAT test[1], I passed, gained admission into university and never looked back. This major boost to my confidence and self-esteem – just to be accepted – was indescribable!

A TAFE (Technical and Further Education) nursing diploma was the first qualification I finished. This was a huge and very important step in rebuilding myself. As a single mum I found many educational goals became too large, or unachievable, or the employment outcomes were poor. Degree courses required more time commitment: three to four years full-time or six to eight years part-time. I found the unstructured freelance style of university learning was very hard for me to navigate while raising two small children, particularly as a single parent with a trauma background.

The highly structured style of adult applied learning at TAFE with two years of full-time commitments was more achievable for my circumstances. Completing this first qualification was the major stepping stone toward me creating my new career pathway and lifestyle. From then, I became healthily addicted to learning… and to finishing.

It took many long hard years to complete my first degree part-time. But when I did, I cried for days.

Education not only elevated my knowledge, employability and income, it lifted *me* as a human being – a survivor of extreme violence and trauma. I evolved from feeling crushed, suffocating deep in the ashes of self-doubt with no identity, to feeling valued, worthy, and extremely proud.

MY FIRST PERPETRATOR, the one who destroyed this beautiful young teenage girl, finally died… several decades after being diagnosed with 'terminal' cancer. Never trust a predator – they believe their own lies.

I cannot adequately express the deep relief of no longer having to look over my shoulder, constantly worrying that I'm being followed, stalked, watched, perved on, that my house might be broken into, that I might be attacked, or my children might be abducted – all that is now *finally* a thing of the past.

But tell my body that. After decades of continual hypervigilance, fear and stress, I remain very unwell with autoimmune diseases, and still have a dire fear of men.

Needing to wear clothes that only *he* approved of, being constantly criticised about how I looked… my face, my hair, my body. Too fat, too ugly, too revealing, too flirty, too slutty, too dowdy. Worrying about everything I said, how I walked and moved, how I looked at him or others. Self-questioning every single thing I did. This was how I was conditioned by his brutality, and this practice of deep self-criticism and constant self-doubt and self-checking has stayed with me.

Since his death, I have taken my name back, my family name; I am visible once more. I am back on the electoral role; I exist again as a citizen. I can celebrate my birth identity – something that had been suppressed, crushed and hidden for decades. I can travel to whatever states and towns I like, and no longer fear seeing him. Finally, I can allow my healing to begin, for I never felt safe while he was alive, especially once I discovered my own mother was the one letting him know where I lived.

My proudest moment was graduating recently as a Doctor of Philosophy (PhD). As I received my third degree, I felt proud of my meaningful research into PTSD and intergenerational family violence.

My family and domestic violence (FDV) story started at birth, witnessing the intense violence of my parents. My first intimate partner DV story began at 15, powerless, unassertive, naïve, depressed, holding no hope. My second DV story, a marriage with children, saw me become suicidal, medicated and crushed.

But my life story continued to manifest. I pursued my dreams through education. I have been married now for over twenty years to a safe, loving and supportive man.

My message of hope to you is that you *will* be free, emotionally, physically, and spiritually. That you *will* be in your dream job. You *will* be in your dream home with your dream partner.

What it takes is a big commitment to Your Self – determination, dedication, discipline, patience, self-love and time. Lots of time. You *will* get there. I did!

STUDY: YOUR STEPPING STONE TO BEING YOU

I used STUDY as my golden ticket for personal growth and development and to find out who I am. Being accepted to study at TAFE and then completing my degree was a major boost to my confidence and self-esteem. Study elevated my knowledge, employability and increased

my income. I felt valued, worthwhile, and proud of myself.

You too can step onto the stepping stones of study to rebuild your life after coercive control.

S—Self-love can help you to counter any negative self-talk. Be kind to yourself, speak to yourself like you would speak to a friend you hold dear. Self-love will help you nurture growth, respect and forgiveness for yourself. Self-love is a foundation for you to heal. Give yourself some self-love. You are worth it.

T—Time: Rebuilding your life after coercive control takes time. It is a big commitment. Give yourself the time needed. Healing takes different amounts of time for each person. There is no fixed time frame for healing. Go at your own pace, one step at a time.

U—Understanding: Study and education can help you to understand yourself, other people, their motives and their behaviours. Study can help you to define you, what you like and dislike and why.

D—Determination, dedication, discipline are the three Ds of a mindset needed to achieve success. You will draw upon these three Ds to keep you moving forward to you and your new life.

Y—Your Self: It's time to focus on your self. What do you want? Who are you? Do you want to take back your name? Wear the clothes that make you feel like you. Be you.

For a downloadable PDF of the checklist above, go to <u>brokentobrilliant.org/coercedtocourageous</u>

CHAPTER 9
OPERATION PHOENIX RISING

'Emerging from the other side of a garbage fire of a relationship, I am making more of an effort to slow down and smell the roses. Life is short, and there is a whole world out there to enjoy.'

As the sharp sounds of gunfire ring out over the firing range, I feel centred and my thoughts are clear. There is something so exhilarating about live-fire training. The smell of gunpowder mixed with the dry eucalyptus scent of the summer heat fills the air. I listen for the pinging sound the bullets make as they hit their metal target. Anticipation and excitement grows. Each shot I take, a gentle squeeze of the trigger, gets me closer to finding out what my final score will be. I close my eyes for a second, open, take a deep breath, then finish my last rounds.

As the training session draws to a close, a stocky safety supervisor who has been monitoring the range yells, 'Make safe, unload,' his deep, husky voice loud and clear over the range. The firing mound erupts with the clicking-on of safety catches, the dropping of ammunition magazines, the metal-on-metal sliding as we cock our weapons open to make sure any chambered rounds are ejected.

I was an officer in the Australian Defence Force. Never did I foresee myself becoming involved in a coercively controlling relationship. I was invincible. I would never fall for such a situation.

But I was wrong. Very wrong.

I am a survivor of domestic violence.

AT THE BEGINNING, the love bombing was intoxicating. The note-passing at work, the subtle, longing glances at each other, as if we were back at school, trying to catch each other's eye. The relationship was moving at a rapid rate of knots. He chased me hard and made sure he showcased his funny and charming side.

I had never experienced this before. I thought: *This must be love*.

He knew all the right things to say and do. Little did I know this was a ploy to lull me into a false sense of security. To gain as much intel on my weak points as possible and use them as ammo later in the relationship, when I was at my weakest, and force me into submission.

DUE TO THE nature of defence life, I was working long hours and away from home quite a bit. So, when I returned, I would always downplay his bad behaviours. Those little things that you shouldn't brush aside. Veiled comments. Him taking my computer off me to prevent me doing work, so I was forced to give him attention.

Things that would be deemed red flags, I put down to him having a bad day or him 'just joking'. Sometimes I would believe he was doing it because he 'loved me'.

Any of my achievements were met with minimal support, if any. Looking back, it was obvious he was jealous of my success both in and out of work.

As the tempo and pressure mounted at work, he grappled for my attention. It was like he was in a competition for it. He needed external validation and subsequently the pressure on me to please him started to rise.

It all became too much and I had a nervous breakdown. The abuse at home then really took off.

I HAD NEVER BEEN EXPOSED to coercion before. I hadn't even heard of it until I left and sought assistance for the abuse.

He was so good at coercive control. Every day became disjointed and left me questioning my sanity. The psychological manipulation did by far more damage than the physical abuse.

Comments like: 'You know I would never lie to you. But I'm just letting you know that you've put on weight.' Then he would slowly proceed to ban me from ordering takeaway and force me out to exercise. He did this believing that, if I lost weight, I would feel better about my body and subsequently be more intimate with him.

He would regularly pressure me to be intimate. 'My love language is physical affection and I NEED it. It's affecting my self-confidence.'

Emotional outbursts were another one of his favourite tactics. He would throw things, punch walls, slam doors and swing from crying to screaming at the drop of a hat.

On a couple of occasions, he came home and said he had told my co-workers about some of the tough and very private things I was going through. When I asked him to respect my privacy, I was met with every manipulative excuse under the sun. 'But they are your friends, and they are asking about you,' or, 'But you're a better liar than me, and it's not fair that you're making me keep secrets.'

By the end, I would be apologising to him because he had no-one to talk to, and my mental health was affecting his self-esteem. Clearly, I was the a-hole. My mistake. I even made psychology appointments for this grown-arse man, as he couldn't be bothered taking responsibility for his poor behaviour.

I felt my spirit was being forced into submission. Like the scene of Aslan the lion on the sacrificial stone in *The Lion, the Witch and the Wardrobe*. My spirit and freedoms were stripped away, one by one, slowly but surely. Simple things like choosing what to wear or even the people I could be friends with were monitored and restricted. My basic freedoms to travel were supressed, and I was even guilted into abandoning my fitness training.

One of the most disempowering things I had to go through was, when I moved in with him, I was forced to give all my household items away, so we didn't have 'double-ups of every-thing'. My pets were locked out of the bedroom at night, even though they had slept on the end of my bed for over ten years. It broke my heart to hear them crying on the other side of the door.

THE NIGHT it got physical is a night I will never forget.

For weeks on end, when I tried to go to bed early he would stand at the door and complain, yell and threaten to leave. He was sleep-depriving me, an abusive tactic to exhaust me and erode my defences further.

One night, I was in bed; he was standing at the door shouting and crying. I said, 'I can't do this anymore,' and rolled over to face away from him.

This enraged him. He slammed the door so hard that it nearly came off the hinges. The door frame buckled under the pressure and white paint flecks scattered all over the timber floor, like the start of the new snow season.

It was so loud it sounded like an artillery piece going off. For a second, I didn't know where I was and thought I was in contact on the battlefield – I went into flight mode.

I followed him to the next room and begged him to stop slamming doors as he knew that it frightened me. He stared into my soul for half a second, then out of nowhere he erupted and grabbed me and threw me across the room.

As I lay there in a daze, he stood over me, screaming, 'Look what you made me do!' I looked up at him. He was losing it. 'I have never done this to anyone before, how could you make me do this?' he sobbed.

By this point, I had become so sick that I just lay there and thought, *I absolutely deserved this. I am a sh__y partner.*

Even after it got physical, I still believed I was to blame and that I must do better.

WE WENT TO COUPLES COUNSELLING. I was listening to him trying to make the appointment all about him. 'I want the relationship back the way it was at the start.' He meant that he wanted me to serve him like a 1950s housewife. Make him dinner, attend to his every sexual need, clean the house and speak when I was spoken to.

In that moment I became brave enough to tell my side of the story: him punching walls, slamming doors, standing over me and yelling and stonewalling me. I left out the physical abuse, as I felt unsafe to disclose it at that time. The counsellor turned to him and had to ask him three times if this was true.

He sheepishly answered, 'Yeah, but it hasn't happened for like six months now.'

The counsellor then asked, 'Is this new behaviour?'

He said, 'Yes.'

Something clicked in me. He was trying to blame this behaviour on me! No-one gets to their thirties and just starts being emotionally and physically abusive.

After that appointment, I knew something was deeply wrong. When I was alone, I called Relationships Australia for advice. After listening to elevator music for around five minutes, a lady answered my call. I explained to her what was going on as I couldn't work out what was happening to me.

She replied in a chipper voice, 'Oh that's easy! You are in a coercive and emotionally manipulative relationship.'

Sh__.

AFTER YEARS of gaslighting and coercive control, I didn't trust my own judgement.

'What if I'm making it up in my head?'

'What if I have this all wrong and I'm just blowing things out of proportion?'

'What if I'm crazy, like he says I am?'

That first call was probably one of the biggest hurdles to get over. But when I was met with a kind, non-judgemental female on the end of the line, I finally felt heard, that my feelings were validated. She helped me understand that what I was going through was wrong and, most importantly, not my fault.

We then came up with a safety plan and she gave me the number for a 24-hour phone service dedicated to domestic violence (DV).

I received more validation from the second phone service. We started planning how I could safely leave. I was directed to moving companies that could assist with my escape, and other assistance such as group and individual DV counselling. I started reading books and listening to podcasts to better understand what

I had gone through, and what I could do to better educate myself to see red flags in the future.

The silver lining was a growing understanding of what coercive control is and how perpetrators operate. I became more confident that I did not cause this, and it was not my fault.

AND THEN THE 'HOOVERING' starts.

As soon as he could feel me pulling away, he used every move he could think of to stop me leaving him. Even to the extent where he tried to convince me to go to a wedding convention with him to plan our future!

This is where relationships can get dangerous.

To leave a very unsafe situation, I had to lie my arse off. I had to sell the idea that I wanted to go back to dating and live in separate accommodation to bring the romantic spark back. A Living Apart Together (LAT) lifestyle.

I arranged to move to a secure complex. I installed cameras. I didn't give him a key.

MOVING DAY ARRIVED. It was time to pick up the keys to my new place. As I anxiously shuffled through the folder of papers I had to sign, a wave of internal panic washed over me. I held my breath. 'Am I making the right decision?' The fear of the unknown began to set in.

I arrived at the new place in the late afternoon and let myself in. It was empty and cold. Void of any of the warmth of what used to be a family home. A shell. A blank canvas if you will, to restart my life over again.

As I walked around in a daze, I found myself in the main

bedroom. It was early spring, and the air started to get a chill in it as the sun set.

I collapsed to the ground overcome with emotions.

I rolled over onto my back, starring up at the ceiling, tears quietly rolling down my face. 'Why the f__k am I not happy? I'm free! I should be happy.'

I discovered it's not like in the movies where you breathe a sigh of relief and start a new life once you're out. Your healing journey is only just beginning. It is a shock to the system when your emotions don't match up with how you think you should be feeling.

FROM THE TIME I realised and fully accepted that I was in a coercive relationship, I was out within five weeks. But if I am being honest, I would have had no problem being homeless if it meant I was out safe. I've had to do it before, and I would do it again.

Once I got out, I deliberately became the most boring person I could be, to make it his idea to end it. It was hard work, slowly cutting contact and making excuses not to catch up – 'I'm working' or 'I'm volunteering'.

His ego was so desperate for reassurance that he needed to find a new supply of affection and admiration asap. He had a new one already lined up as soon as we separated.

Perfect for me. But bad luck for her.

SOMETHING THAT HELPED me move past this garbage fire of a 'relationship' was to take charge of my health in a multifaceted way. This included cleaning up my nutrition, moving my body in meaningful ways, engaging in as many different counselling (DV specific), psychology and psychiatry sessions as possible, getting better sleep habits in place, keeping a gratitude journal, and learning as much as I could about toxic/coercive relationships and how to avoid them in the future.

I have also spent time with a careers counsellor to really nail down what I want to achieve in my life. What makes me excited to get out of bed every day? What aligns with my morals and ethics?

A skill that really helped me get through this healing phase was to reframe my experience in the relationship. Instead of continuing to replay and relive what was done and feel powerless, I reframed it as: What did I learn from this? What can I take away from this experience and use it to better myself as a member of society?

Most importantly, this type of thinking allows me to take back MY power and reduce time spent feeling like a victim. To me, any time spent in a victim state robs me of precious time to move forward as a victor over my life and my destiny.

Is life different to what it was before the relationship?

Yes.

Am I grateful for what I have been through?

Yes.

No-one should be treated that way. Ever. But the experiences I went through have made me the person I am today. Yes, I am still trying to find who the real me is, but I am stronger because of the journey so far.

I know what I will and won't tolerate in my life. My true friends stayed by my side. But I also gained new ones along the way. Friends that I probably would never have had the privilege of meeting any other way. And for that, I am also grateful.

Emerging from the other side of a garbage fire of a relationship, I am making more of an effort to slow down and smell the roses. Life is short, and there is a whole world out there to enjoy. Such simple things – like lying in the sun with my pets and reading a book, or a spur-of-the-moment road trip with friends – are important to me.

I am more confident to speak up when my needs are not being met. If something is making me uncomfortable, I say so. If I don't want to go somewhere, I don't. I am more confident in my abilities to enforce my boundaries, and not be swayed to deviate from that. I now have the clarity to cut any unnecessary BS from my life that is not adding positively to it.

That guilt trip isn't working here, baby!

Hot tips to leave sinking relation-ships – safely:

- Get coloured copies of all your important documents. Keep the originals somewhere safe, like a trusted family member's place.
- Make up a go-bag with a change of clothes and keep it at a trusted person's house. Don't forget a bag for the pets.
- Every pay I would withdraw $50 cash when I was checking out of the supermarket. That escape money was hidden away if I ever needed it. And I did.
- Make sure there is no spyware on your phone.
- If you need a protection notice[1] in place, a police officer, lawyer, friend or family member can apply for one for you or you can apply for one yourself. Seek assistance from the police. It is their job to protect you from the perpetrator.
- I started documenting incidents in my daily paper diary in code, or even documenting simple things

such as car services etc. This saved my bacon later when he would go on to make up malicious lies about me to the police.

- I also kept documents/photos/screenshots on my phone in a hidden calculator app.
- If you put WiFi cameras up, rename them as a gaming console or a music device. It's not hard to sit out the front of a house and run the WiFi to see if there are cameras up.

I SIT IN A FARAWAY LAND, surrounded by ancient ruins, and just stare out over the snow-capped mountain range. The air is fresh and has a sharpness to it. I am lost for words and overcome with emotion. For the first time in a long time, maybe even for the first time, I feel emotionally, physically and spiritually connected with the world.

I never thought I would do my first solo travel in a country where English isn't the first language. I have made so many friends along the way from all over the world. This is the bittersweet part of this experience: to connect with people in such a short period of time and then have to say goodbye. I hope I will cross paths with them again one day, but I know that will probably never happen. But it is the impermanence of these moments that make these experiences so magical.

I don't want to take anything for granted. In the awareness of the limited time we have together, we are able to be open-minded and curious with the world.

The journey of life has led me to this spot. Right here, right now, I am truly free.

TAKE CHARGE OF YOUR LIFE

To move forward away from the abusive relationship, take CHARGE of your life. I was able to do this through counselling, healthy habits, acceptance, reframing, gratitude, and education. You too can emerge out the other side of the garbage fire, to smell the roses and make the most of every moment. *Life is short, and there is a whole world out there to enjoy.* Take CHARGE – it is your life to live.

C—Counselling: This is a confidential talk therapy where you can share your concerns with a trained professional who is non-judgemental. Their role is to help you work through the issues, and support you to problem solve and develop tools and skills to deal with any issues. There are many different professionals you can seek help from including counsellors, psychotherapists, psychiatrists, and careers counsellors. It is important that you feel comfortable, safe, and supported and that you are moving forward in your sessions.

H—Healthy habits: What are the healthy habits you need? Reflect on your day; do you get 30 minutes of exercise? Do you eat foods that are not refined and as close to nature as possible? Do you take time to do mindfulness or meditation? Are you learning tools to reduce anxiety? Reflect on your health habits and make one change at a time. Once that change is embedded, move to the next change. Be kind to yourself.

A—Acceptance: This means accepting what is out of your personal control. For example, you are unable to control how another person behaves. How you feel may not align with what you or society expects, such as being happy after leaving. Accept where you are and how you are feeling and focus on making changes that move you forward.

R—Reframe: You can reframe the situation by looking at the positives or you can look at the evidence of your situation compared to your interpretation and thoughts about it. From what you have been through, ask: What did I learn from this? What can I take away from this experience and use it to better myself as a member of society? How can what I have been through help others?

G—Gratitude: Gratitude is the appreciation of what is valuable and meaningful to oneself – being thankful and appreciative. Being grateful takes time and daily action, such as keeping a gratitude journal or taking gratitude photos or writing a letter of thanks and reading it to the person you are grateful for. Practising gratitude does not stop you feeling loss, anger and frustration. Practising gratitude helps to stop the wallowing victimhood and helps you to take charge of your life.

E—Education: Use books, podcasts and courses to increase your understanding of what you have been through: domestic violence, coercive control, narcissistic behaviour, toxic relationships. This will help you to stop blaming yourself, to understand that you were not able to change the abuser's behaviour. Educating yourself will also help you to understand what is a safe, healthy and trusting relationship so you can identify and choose such relationships in the future.

For a downloadable PDF of the checklist above, go to [brokentobril liant.org/coercedtocourageous](http://brokentobrilliant.org/coercedtocourageous)

CHAPTER 10
FREE FROM SHAME

'I have learnt that shame does not belong to me. The shame that for years kept me anchored to his abuse does not live here.'

The drizzling rain has me on my toes as I drive home after a long day of classes. In front of me, the four-wheel drive vehicle travelling at eighty kilometres per hour slows to a sudden and unexpected stop, getting ready to make a right-hand turn into a driveway. I stop my car behind his.

My head slams against the driver-side window. The taste of blood fills my mouth. The radio console flies from the dashboard and lands on the passenger floor.

Glass smashes. My chin hits the top of the steering wheel. My knees crash against the underside of the steering wheel.

I know this pain and chaos.

My first thought is to keep myself safe. Brace myself. Flashbacks of fear.

I push the thoughts away. I need to focus on what is happening. I scan the road. No, this is not the same as being chased and run off the road while attempting an escape.

This is an accident.

~

'I thought I'd killed you,' spurts the young man, the driver of the car that hit me.

'I think I'm fine.' I say nothing more. I am not clear where I am or what has happened, but I know silence is safer than antagonism. Another familiar memory.

We stand beside my car, which sits squashed between two vehicles in the middle of the highway.

I see lengths of wood scattered on the road. The same wood that flew from the roof of the car that hit me, through my back window, hitting the dashboard and flying back out. I inch my hands into my pockets so the driver, who I learn is Dan, can't see them shaking. Another old habit.

I fidget with my hair, my hands. I twirl my fingers in my pockets. I clench my mouth shut, waiting, waiting for the punch that usually came, the one that blindsided me so often.

He has been dead 37 years, yet this fear still triggers when I least expect it.

~

My life is frantically busy. I make myself busy. I leave no minute of the day with space where abusive thoughts and words can run through my head. Most of the time this works well – until there is an accident like this one.

My working week involves intense teaching and training across two tertiary settings. The roles are demanding. One role involves a behaviour change program for people who have tested positive for illicit substances while in charge of a vehicle. Each session, I am ready for their behaviours. These people are angry and resentful, and believe they are hard done by. I am not intimidated by the loud voices, the scraping chairs, the constant movement. I have heard these words of abuse, intended to keep me in line, many times before. These participants take no responsibility for their actions; the blame belongs to someone else; someone else made them do it.

Hours of personal development stand me in good stead. I have developed the skill of pausing rather than reacting. I withstand the eight-hour sessions, braced for anything thrown at me.

On the day of the accident, I attend classes as a student. I am studying an extra qualification in vocational education. I am a lifelong learner. At night, I write and research my own essays for my study, as well as creating resources to support my delivery of training.

The intensity I create around my work ensures my tears are always kept at bay. Self-control is important to me. I keep my emotions and reactions contained tightly against my chest. My body is held rigid in protective mode.

As I look at my crushed car, I think to myself, *I don't have time to get this fixed*. Which really means I am now exposed – without a car and without work.

THE CAR CRASH triggers my PTSD, something I have kept under control for the past 15 years. The Transport Accident Commission recognises my trauma and agrees to pay for counselling. I find a therapist after much trial and error. She understands PTSD and hears me as I speak about my passion for work and to achieve success. She allows me to ramble – some may say 'to avoid'.

She hears my grief over the loss of my ability to work. I mourn the loss. I waste hours staring into space, recalling the joy and safety I felt in front of a class or managing a department in a large TAFE, or launching a new educational project for consumers of drug and alcohol treatment services. A project I developed and wrote myself. Holding onto my career and staying in the workforce is important to me.

Suddenly, my choice for a working life has been stolen by a car accident.

Therapy is wholistic, focusing on personal relationships as well as returning to driving. The therapist questions why, as a widow, I am not dating. My response is flippant.

'I am happy working, dancing with friends and being with my kids and grandson – plus I couldn't be bothered picking up someone else's socks.'

She suggests homework between sessions using the guidelines of Acceptance and Commitment Therapy. This provides an opportunity for me to try actions aligned with my values.

My therapist directs me to focus on my self-talk and take action to make change. My self-talk slips into: I don't deserve to be happy; I am not entitled to be selfish or choose enjoyable activities.

I have pushed my past deep below the centre of the earth.

She asks, 'Where do you think you developed these beliefs? You are smart, funny, a leader, a perfectionist at work, yet you don't believe you are worthy of happiness. You seem to be telling me you are to blame for all that happened. Where does that thinking come from?'

She suggests awakening my soul by finding ways to please myself. This activates unsettling memories. Media discussions at the time raise issues about the rights of women to have control over their own bodies. This activates more deeply-buried, unsettling memories.

She notices a change in my language. Instead of my flippant comments about him I start to say, 'He was controlling, demanding, selfish. He dominated my life with his demands and wants.' I say these words but I feel no connection to them or to him. I respond as an automaton.

She tells me I have been disassociating to endure the trauma.

Who was he, this man who took over my life?

He works hard by day and indulges his ego singing in bands at night. I meet him at a popular pub in a trendy inner-city suburb. He is singing in the band.

At the end of the night, he asks me if I want to go for a hamburger. I say yes. The hamburger is delicious; he talks nonstop about himself and his singing. It is 1977 and men rarely wear earrings, but he does. His hair is held tight with hairspray, and he is wearing make-up. In fact, he is wearing more make-up than I am.

When he drives me back to where I parked, we sit in his car and talk a little bit more, and then he asks, 'Can I see you again?'

I explain. 'No, not really. I'm busy selling my house, packing up and sorting what I will do. My plan is to travel overseas all of 1978, for the full 12 months. I have travel leave from my work organised. And I will be catching up with my friend. Travelling overland on the hippy trail.'

'Where do you live? You know, the house you are selling?' he asks, as if I hadn't spoken.

He wears me down, he is persistent. In the end I say, 'I'm sure I'll be back to see the band and we can catch up then.'

As I am climbing out of his sports car, he grabs my elbow firmly and says, 'You gotta at least let me ring you. What's your number? I'll give ya a call.'

I recite my number quickly, never imagining for a minute he will remember. I push his door shut, returning to my car parked across the road and driving home, not giving him another thought.

From that point on I am never free of him.

No-one I have dated or been in a relationship with has ever behaved like him. At first, I joke to friends about him ringing, about him parking out the front of my house or my work, about him following me in the car.

We aren't dating, I don't like him. One hamburger was more than enough.

He 'love bombs' me. Flowers on the doorstep, lunch dropped at my work because he has followed me there and knows the location. He skips in, joyful and playful, and at first my co-workers think he is cute! Then it becomes creepy. The all-day sitting in his car, watching; the phone calls; the notes slipped under the door.

I had planned to stay with my parents after my house sold. My house sells and for the few months until my travel departure, I move to his place on nine acres of land.

I possess a large dog and a cat; he convinces me my animals can stay on his acreage. I can rent one of the spare bedrooms. I can store my car and furniture in the large sheds when I travel.

This move revolves around being friends, tenants in common, having our own space. We will continue doing what we usually do, and my rent will help with rental of the property.

It seems like the perfect arrangement. Housemates.

THINGS CHANGE QUICKLY.

His hands grab my throat, squeezing it tight, lifting me off the wet shower floor. I struggle against him, trying to pry his hands away. Then he drops me and walks away.

I know I must get out of this house. I quickly dress. The phone is disconnected. I grip my car keys tight as I call my dog and pick up my cat, making my way to the front door.

I can now see my car; the front driver-side wheel lies on the ground.

There is no-one to tell and nowhere to go for help.

Silence; politeness; covering the bruises on my neck. I keep to myself till Monday when I can drive to work and not come back.

My car will not start. Work is important and my salvation. The only car available to drive is his sports car. If I drive it, I will have to bring it back later that day. If I don't, I am trapped in his house all day. The phone has disappeared altogether. This time he has taken the entire handset with him, not just pulled the wiring out.

I count the weeks until I will be flying out of Australia. My self-talk is a constant mantra of 'not long now, not long now'.

My belongings begin to disappear. He jokes I don't need make-up or tight jeans. That his mother is enjoying reading the books I left on the shelf.

I wake one night to him masturbating on my face. I am repulsed but remain silent. My eyes sting, flaring red and impossible to hide. Who do I tell?

It isn't long before he begins telling me I have no real friends. That the ones I have only use me, and I am too stupid to know.

'No-one rings you, do they?' he says thrusting his finger into my collarbone. I discover he answers the phone, takes messages, and never passes them on to me.

My space is no longer my space. My bed becomes his bed. Consent is not consent. Fear drives every concession I make. Fear he will hurt me and fear he will carry out the threats against my family that are being made more often.

'Won't take much to kill them. Just one punch under the nose.' He laughs as if that is funny.

I never use my voice to stop him humiliating me. He silences groups of people with his degrading comments. He drags me onto his knee and pretends I am a ventriloquist doll, and he speaks.

Today, my voice is powerful and would silence him, or more, so he would never get me on his knee.

∾

THEN HIS STORIES of woe begin, his time in Vietnam, his poverty-stricken home life, his father leaving him and – the cruncher – that he can never have children as he is sterile from a childhood surgery. Foolishly, I decide to give my body a rest from the pill.

My right to consent or refuse sex is dismissed. He makes light of it, as if having sex means nothing but pleasure.

A pregnancy from being tricked delays my trip. He delights that I have fallen for his trick but is not so delighted when I seek an abortion. The violence escalates. The death threats are directed. He smashes the headlights on my father's new car.

MY PARENTS DRIVE me to the airport. I have my ticket and passport. I am leaving – six months after my initial plan.

I believe I am free as I hug my friend in London. I become me again. We talk about books we have read, world problems and how to solve them, future travel plans, music. I laugh without fear.

After six weeks travelling north to Scotland I return to London and walk into Victoria House to pick up my mail and there he is, sitting, waiting. I think, 'He will not kill me here.'

His death threats scare me, and I have nowhere to turn for help in the 1970s. Not the police, not any women's services. There is nothing.

FOR EIGHT YEARS until his death, I whisper each day, 'I hope you die today.'

When the police tell me he has been killed in a workplace accident, I freeze, believing they will know I wished him dead.

Weeks later, the police interview me, asking questions about his work equipment and what he was doing that day. I am riddled with guilt.

Can they tell by looking at me that I wished him dead?

I fall headfirst into survival mode, terrified a dreadful joke is being played and he could walk through the door at any minute.

Eleven days later I give birth to our third child. I am a widow at 32 years of age, with three children under the age of five. I love my children in a way I cannot find the words to describe. (The promise he would no longer be violent if I 'gave' him children was never honoured.)

I protect him. I push away every memory of the abuse. I laugh and say I can buy new things this week without him spending all the money.

I start my own business until the third baby starts school. I go back to university and begin work as a learning consultant. I learn to drive his new car that I cannot sell because of the loan he has set up.

I have an income, a car in my name, insurance in my name, my bank accounts, and my house. I play squash one night a week with friends, who entertain the kids while I am on the court. I begin spiritual and personal development, exploring who I am without being truthful about those eight years that traumatised me, hurt me, but did not break me.

I study Women's Studies, making new friends and solidifying my feminist views. My return to work is as though I have not been away.

I make a promise to myself to learn as much as I can, to grab all opportunities for training and new skills.

My qualifications and capability are recognised.

I am comfortable training teachers, delivering research that I have undertaken and assisting schools to develop drug and alcohol strategies.

My eldest son shows signs of trauma which he expresses through drug and alcohol use. I can never bring myself to admit he has witnessed the violence, he has heard the stomping and yelling, he has seen the car driven at me, he has cleaned the blood from my face.

My son dies of an overdose without ever having a conversation with me about what he saw.

AT TIMES I REMAIN COERCED, in the grips of his abuse even though he is dead.

I train students to work in this sector without disclosing my own story. I believe I am a good teacher because I can explore the complexity and depth. Disassociating allows me to perform as the educator, the manager who holds knowledge without revealing my story. When the walls fall down, his coercion continues to torment me.

I want to shout: How did a carefree spirit, intelligent, curious about the world, a lover of loud bands, Bob Dylan and the ocean, end up trapped?

I KNOW the warning signs now. I know the seriousness of those signs. I know that good-looking singers in a band are just as likely to be abusers as any other person.

As the years pass, I master the brush cutter – I can even replace the spark plug, the wire, the blade. I can cut metre-high grass. I can restore old furniture.

I inspire others to be the best they can be. I learn that drugs, or the condition of addiction, are cruel.

I find my voice. I volunteer to facilitate support groups for families. I fight against the stigma that surrounds families and drug use, to the point that I receive an award in recognition.

I must look inside and find myself. I know I am in there and I know I am a decent person. I am smarter than him, funnier than him, driven to be successful. I discover I like myself – all four feet eleven inches of me.

I train myself to listen when people make positive comments about me and about my kids. I wear make-up, I dye my hair magenta, I can look like a hippie one day and an old nana the next. I choose.

I wish I had known the me I am now when he controlled my life. I would have asked for help, I would have kept asking for help, from police, his burly friends, the band members. I would have kept driving my car as fast as I could away from him. He would never have run me off the road.

I would be telling me that I am magnificent, that I am strong, that I can walk away, that I will not be intimidated by his threats because who I am is enough. I would tap into my now-developed problem-solving abilities and make plans, create supports, have a bank account and cash in a safe place away from him. I would have a second phone. I would tell trusted friends my plans. I would also ask those same friends to check in on me.

I accept this as domestic violence and I will no longer protect his story or fabricate one that makes me feel less ashamed.

I have learnt that the shame does not belong to me. The shame that for years kept me anchored to his abuse does not live here anymore.

FREE FROM SHAME

The shame of the coercive controlling situation and hiding it from the world was finally broken open by the triggering car accident. I had to deal with the suppressed emotion of intense negative self-judgment and viewing myself as worthless. With the help of a trauma-informed therapist, I was able to work through my past trauma and FREE myself of shame. I reflected on all that I have achieved. By recognising all the steps I took to be FREE, rebuilding my life after abuse and seeking support, I was able to let go of the abuse. You too can be FREE by following these steps and seeking support.

F—Financial management and freedom: Begin to manage your financial situation, set up bank accounts, ensure you have insurance. Finding yourself free and able to make your own choices might be daunting in the beginning but each time you stand up straight and venture into the world you will feel stronger and free of shame. Freedom to make choices can be as simple as deciding to savour your coffee in the sunshine or invite a friend around to taste the biscuits you have made. Being free of fear takes courage.

R—Recognition: As a trauma survivor, receiving compliments can be very hard as we feel so unworthy. Recognition and compliments may be triggering because in the past you may have been used to thinking: what comes next? It is important to learn how to genuinely accept a compliment, to be recognised for your worth and value. Notice how you may quickly deflect a compliment. Train yourself to accept a compliment. Stop next time you receive a compliment. Pause, breathe in deeply, and say a simple thank you with a smile. Keep practising. It is also recommended that you work on self-acceptance and seeing your worth with your counsellor or psychologist.

E—Education and Employment: Become a lifelong learner, educate yourself, gain qualifications. Through education you will learn more about yourself and it will enable you to seek employment. Employment can build your self-confidence and create financial freedom, helping to break the cycle of abuse.

E—Empower others: You can empower others through your own actions and attitude. Be the best you, learning new things such as how to use garden machinery, undertake car maintenance, restore old furniture, or fix a leaking tap. Give back to others by volunteering for a charity or being a part of a support group.

For a downloadable PDF of the checklist above, go to <u>brokentobrilliant.org/coercedtocourageous</u>

CHAPTER 11
THE IMPACT OF WRITING MY STORY

Several authors from our previous books *Broken to Brilliant*, *Terror to Triumph* and *Shattered to Shining* joined us at the *Coerced to Courageous* writing workshop. They shared with the authors of our fourth book the impact of sharing their story in our previous books. Here are their stories of how they have journeyed away from abuse and rebuilt their lives. They express the gain they have found in the pain, new lives filled with self-love, healing and personal growth, and a strong voice.

SELF-DOUBT TO SELF-LOVE, AND LETTING GO OF SHAME AND BLAME

When I think back to the start of my experiences with Broken to Brilliant, I see a very different version of myself to the woman who now exists.

Arriving at our writing workshop I walked in shakily, feeling apprehensive, fragile and fearful. Despite living through years of abuse and turmoil, I was drenched in self-doubt that I had a story to tell, let alone one that might help others. I was unaware as that weekend unfolded of the dramatic change my life would move through over the next few years.

Meeting fellow authors showed me that I was not alone in the thriving journey. I was immediately surrounded by support and understanding. Since stepping out of shame to write my story, I have grown and transformed in so many ways. Being an author with Broken to Brilliant helped me see my worth and to understand the depths of what I went through so that I could find ways to move forward in life.

I am more confident and feel comfortable with who I am. I let go of blame and shame to be a better mother, partner, colleague, friend and woman.

In my career, I have become a better worker than ever before as I grew in self-assurance to build genuine relationships with colleagues and clients. I have considerably increased my earning capacity and skillset. No longer hiding in my past, my life experiences inspire a strong, solution-focused work ethic. I model strength and resilience to those I work alongside.

My involvement with Broken to Brilliant has expanded my life experiences and developed new capabilities in many ways. I have participated in multiple self-development courses. I've had the opportunity to contribute to domestic violence facilitation courses, to fundraise, to speak at community events, to present and write in blogging groups, to develop my emotional communication skills and to mentor fellow victim-survivors. Being part of the Broken to Brilliant community has opened up connections and pathways that have made me a better person.

Now I turn up for my children with confidence and trust that my maternal instincts are heartfelt and that I make the right choices for their future. I gained the knowledge and ability to build my finances. I bought a light-filled unit by the ocean that was a peaceful haven for us to heal and feel safe together. I also purchased a new car that was reliable and budget friendly so that there were even leftover funds to enrol the kids into activities they enjoyed and thrived in.

I found the courage to take up old hobbies that interested me, such as reading, cooking, gardening and bushwalking once more. I accepted invitations from family and friends that I had become used to declining. I asked for help when I needed it. I trained willingly again after signing up for fun-runs and joining a local sporting team, which has been a fun source of support and fitness.

Self-care became a new focus after I realised that my happiness was not a selfish goal. I took time to seek therapies and to look within to heal deep hurts and trauma. I learnt how to set healthy boundaries and to manage long term suffering and disease so that my body can recover and repair. I recognised that I had to be at my best to find the best in life.

I have a deep knowing that my children and I are now safe and that we can be a loving and loyal family for each other. That growth has blossomed into a new love for me with a gentle and kind partner. Now we all enjoy a bigger home that we have built together in the country, surrounded by fresh air, space and birdsong. We are excitedly planning a celebration of our love with a joyful wedding in our backyard with close friends and family in the near future.

I have stopped apologising for myself. I have a life I am proud of with a new happiness that is worth celebrating. I wake each day with optimism and feel grateful for the tumultuous experiences of my past. Without those and without my journey with Broken to Brilliant, I would not have discovered this version of myself where I am brave, beautiful, strong, capable and worthy.

THE HARD AND REWARDING WORK OF POST-TRAUMATIC GROWTH

Telling my story helped me to understand myself, where I came from, where I want to go and what is most important to me. Sharing my experience and pain helped me to release that part of my life and move forward. The chapters of what happened to me were closed. I felt like I moved completely beyond my anger, blame and victimhood and into the part of my life where I could take full responsibility for myself as an individual and as a parent.

While I had made peace with the earlier chapters of my life regarding my childhood and my marriage, I realised I was still drowning in the grief from the guilt I held for my children's pain and suffering. Although still a work in progress, I have spent the last three years learning to accept and let go of what I can't control, and to forgive myself. This included understanding that I don't have any control over my children – only influence. What is within my control is to use my influence in a way that hopefully leads them toward taking responsibility for themselves, for them to choose healing and truly break the cycle of abuse and dysfunction.

Since writing my story three years ago, I have continued to expand my knowledge with an uncountable number of hours of research and, of course, life experience. I have also spent over 150 hours attending and presenting at conferences as well as doing various training and workshops. I have absorbed much knowledge around domestic violence and coercive control; chronic and complex trauma and mental health; respectful relationships and communication. I have also gained skills in dialectical behavioural therapy; art and alternative therapies; and program development and facilitation.

Although my caring responsibilities for my children with mental illness take up most of my time, I also make the time to do small amounts of work in various spaces. I co-facilitate a healing program, helping empower women and their children affected by domestic abuse. I provide Carer Peer Support in a therapy group with parents and young people with mental illness. I also co-facilitate programs with young children for social and emotional learning and prevention of domestic abuse.

While I have continued to learn, I have also continued to work on my personal post-traumatic growth (PTG). This is hard work, and sometimes very painful, but the reward is amazing. When you grow beyond your trauma you are able to see every 'failure' as another opportunity to learn and grow. I believe this is where incredible wisdom can be gained from the 'lived experience'. This is where lies the passion and purpose that can come from the pain.

The most important lessons I have learnt over the last ten years of growth would be:

1. Recovery and rebuilding have no time frame. Just keep going. Every step takes time, but keep investing that time in yourself because you are worth it and you deserve to heal.

2. It's important to find a safe way to externalise your story. Staying in it reinforces the pain, rather than releasing it. Express your pain in words, written or spoken, or through art, movement, music or therapy. Just find a way to release yourself from its grip. It will then truly no longer define you.

3. *Every* change starts from *within*. It's the inner work that matters the most. Self-connection, self-awareness, self-compassion, self-forgiveness, self-care, self-love. When you first have these things for yourself, you can truly experience and appreciate them from others.

4. As a parent, grandparent, partner, daughter, friend, or any other hat that you wear, recognise and let go of what is not within your control. You don't have

control over anyone, but you do have influence. The capacity for a strong influence comes from a strong sense of *self* and modelling that strength.

5. To take full responsibility for your own life is to take your power back. It is incredibly important to set healthy boundaries, learn how to respond instead of react, and learn to accept what cannot be changed.

I look back at the past chapters of my life and I am proud of how far I have come. I am grateful for the knowledge and wisdom and the opportunities for growth.

My current chapter is still not easy (is life ever easy? I don't know), but I have an appreciation of moments of peace and joy that I never had before. The more I connect with who I truly am at a soul-deep level, and live authentically and mindfully, the more comfortable I am in my own skin; the more I love the person that I am; the more compassion and forgiveness I show myself; and the more I can be the best version of myself for everyone, including me.

I see the light at the end of this chapter for all of my continued hard work, and I look forward to the chapter of my life beyond parenting. The chapter that is all about me, continuing to shine my light and helping others to shine theirs.

~

HEALING THE WORLD, ONE WOMAN AT A TIME

I had written off as 'normal behaviour' the relationship I had been in and the emotional and mental abuse I had endured. It was just a part of life, not to be questioned, as I was so enamoured with my partner at the time.

Once I started on my journey of personal development and

met the beautiful Kate Smith, Founding Director of Broken to Brilliant, and shared my story in one of the Broken to Brilliant books, I discovered that this relationship was in fact not a normal relationship but one of mental and emotional abuse. One that I am sure was on the path to becoming physically abusive if I hadn't left the relationship when I did.

Through meeting Kate and sharing my story as a Broken to Brilliant author, I was able to acknowledge the destructive nature of my past relationship.

Awareness was the first key in my healing journey. Whether I was in denial or disbelief I am not sure, but once I acknowledged the relationship for what it was I started to heal.

The second step was sharing my story. Through this reflection I could see how far I had come from the emotionally scarred woman I had been, lacking in confidence and self-esteem. Stepping into my own personal power has truly been life changing.

I have been on a quest of personal development, an avid student of personal development and growth. This quest has included listening to podcasts, attending retreats, reading books, connecting with other likeminded women, and engaging coaches to help me step up into my power. I have continued my journey at Toastmasters, learning to become a confident public speaker.

Today, I have started my own consulting business, created workshops, a networking event, my own podcast, a group coaching program, and high-level one-on-one coaching to help business owners create with confidence the profitable, cash-rich business of their dreams. Without my personal development quest, part of which was sharing my story as a part of the Broken to Brilliant author community, I would not be the woman I have become, achieving all my desires and more.

I spent many years soul searching, clearing my sh__, before I found my now-husband – my loving soulmate who supports me in all that I do. We have been able to welcome our gorgeous daughter who we fought to have through a year-long IVF journey.

I live in my dream home close to the beach and every day I can do what I love.

Since sharing my story, I have had so many wins and successes, my life has truly done a complete 180-degree turn.

I know on reflection that healing my emotional being from the mentally and emotionally abusive relationship I endured for almost my entire twenties has not only impacted the life I am living today, but it is also helping to heal the generational wounds that this trauma has caused, in turn helping to heal my daughter's journey as well.

This past year, I have also started my spiritual journey. As I begin to tap into the power greater than me, I open my heart to more self-love, more love of humanity, greater forgiveness of myself and others, leading me further on my journey of healing.

As a courageous woman sharing your story, I know that for you, too, anything is possible. Once you begin on the path of self-healing and forgiveness, the road to a life of happiness and joy is ahead.

Thank you to all of the courageous women before me, and the courageous women following me. Together we are on a journey to heal ourselves and the world.

I DISCOVERED I HAD A VOICE, AND IT WAS STRONG

I am sitting here, looking out across the water of the man-made lake, on a cloudy, cool autumn day. It's my birthday week, where I celebrate my mid-fifties. I've been reflecting on my journey since I wrote my story of childhood domestic and family abuse.

I had never put pen to paper and explored my writing skills before. Yet, I was ready to share my story in one of Broken to Brilliant's books. A story that had been hidden within me for so long. I had no idea the journey I was about to embark on would lead into some incredible moments of clearness and healing.

I was able to focus on a couple of areas of my story. With the support of my psychologist, I began making sense of the multi-layered abusive environment I grew up in and the impact it had on my life.

It wasn't like: 'Okay, I've written my story and I'm all good now.'

There were many times I faltered and relapsed into what is known as my 'survival mode'. However, with determination and courage I embraced the healing journey.

I discovered I had a voice, and it was strong.

I acknowledged we must bring our voices out into the open and be heard from all directions.

I went on to volunteer on Broken to Brilliant's Research and Education Committee. I completed a thematic analysis of Broken to Brilliant's three books, identifying the top ten strategies to rebuilding your life after domestic and family violence.

The confidence I gained from that journey gave me confidence to show up and co-create the Broken to Brilliant Mentoring Program, including the *Broken to Brilliant Mentoring Journal*.

I've been honoured to be asked to co-present and co-chair at the 2019 Gold Coast Stop Domestic Violence Conference, and participate in various trainings such as facilitator training of the domestic violence program 'Journeys', the Broken to Brilliant Blogging GEMS program, and podcast training.

I've also continued my counselling, healing the very depths of my trauma – and, boy, it has been deep!

I have since learnt that I have dissociative identity disorder.[1]

This is a direct result of the complex trauma I experienced throughout my childhood. I experienced time lapses or changing behaviours along with other traits that were not congruent with my version of myself.

My therapist had been dropping the words 'dissociative identity disorder' (DID) almost from the beginning of our sessions. I thought it was simply in relation to dissociating during sexual events.

Two years later, I said to her, 'I misplace things. I can't remember where or when I put something away. I can't remember people's names. There are complete blanks of time, and a vagueness that's difficult to describe.'

This is when she gently conveyed that what I was experiencing was dissociation. I sat for what felt like an hour but, in reality, was a couple of minutes and it connected…

I have been dissociating my whole life!

Through lots of self-reflection and talking it through in therapy, I began learning what this actually means for me and for us.

In the beginning, I may not have felt I was ready to take on this journey. I even 'hid' from myself and others. I spent time hibernating in what I call 'the nothingness'. The place where you don't feel, you have no words to communicate, you are just 'numb' – not depressed!

I hid 'the nothingness' from others.

Until, one day, I made a bargain and I forced myself out of my bed. I could go back to that place of comfort as long as I did something with my family and was authentically me.

Now, I look for ways I can include my teenage son and do something fun, even if it's for an hour.

I'm continually coming to know who has been in my 'Survival Team' and how all parts of me have contributed to me being here today.

Through this process I realised I'm a writer!

I love to write, sharing my story with others in the hope they find inspiration and gain insight into what they may have experienced, and find one of the strategies I've used beneficial to their healing.

Saying yes to sharing such an important message of the

impact of childhood domestic violence and abuse was an absolute honour.

I was approached to take part as a support person for the four–day writer's workshop for the incredibly brave authors in this extraordinary, insightful book.

I've since co-authored two additional books, my role as a returning author in *Coerced to Courageous* being the third. I've also been accepted as a co-author in an upcoming fourth book… with plans to launch my first solo book next year!

I will be forever grateful for everything that has happened in my life. Although scary and traumatic, it led me to exactly where I am today… thriving!

FREE PRINTABLE CHECKLISTS

Would you like to download a free printable PDF of the checklists that appear at the end of each chapter?

Go to:
brokentobrilliant.org/coercedtocourageous

Or simply point your phone camera at the QR code below.

CONTACT NUMBERS

AUSTRALIA NATIONAL

- 1800 RESPECT (1800 737 732) or reach out via the online chat at https://www.1800respect.org.au. 24-hour national domestic, family and sexual violence counselling, information and support service for any Australian who has experienced, or is at risk of, family and domestic violence and/or sexual assault.
- Lifeline—for any person in Australia who is contemplating suicide, experiencing emotional distress, or caring for someone in crisis: 131 114, national 24-hour number for confidential crisis support, or reach out via text 0477 13 11 14, or chat online at https://www.lifeline.org.au
- Police, Fire or Ambulance: call 000 in a life-threatening emergency for police, fire or ambulance.
- Translating and Interpreting Service—to gain access to an interpreter in your own language (free): phone 131 450 or go to https://www.tisnational.gov.au

- Mensline Australia—supports men and boys who are dealing with family and relationship difficulties: 1300 78 99 78, online chat and video chat at https://mensline.org.au
- Kids Help Line: 1800 551 800 telephone counselling or https://kidshelpline.com.au for email and web counselling for different age groups of children and young people.
- Australian Childhood Foundation—counselling for children and young people affected by abuse: 1800 381 581 or https://www.childhood.org.au
- Relationships Australia—for relationship support services for individuals, families and communities: 1300 364 277 or https://relationships.org.au
- Blue Knot Foundation—support for anyone who is affected by complex trauma: 1300 657 380 Monday–Sunday, 9 am–5 pm AEST or go to https://blueknot.org.au
- National Counselling and Referral Service – Disability —an Australia-wide telephone service that provides emotional support, referrals or information: 1800 421 468, 9 am–6 pm AEST Monday–Friday; 9 am–5 pm AEST Saturday, Sunday and public holidays or go to https://blueknot.org.au/national-counselling-referral-service-disability
- LGBTIQ Qlife—anonymous, free LGBTI peer support and referral for people in Australia wanting to talk about sexuality, identity, gender, bodies, feelings or relationships: 1800 184 527, 3 pm to midnight, every day.
- Reach Out—a safe, anonymous space for young people aged 18–25 to get free, one-to-one support from a trained peer worker: https://au.reachout.com

- Ask Izzy—a free, anonymous website that connects people in need with housing, a meal, money help, family violence support, counselling and much more. Thousands of services listed across Australia: https://askizzy.org.au
- Adults Surviving Child Abuse (ASCA): Find a meeting group at https://www.ascasupport.org
- Brave Hearts—support for child sexual abuse: https://bravehearts.org.au

AUSTRALIAN CAPITAL TERRITORY

- Domestic Violence Crisis Service: 02 6280 0900 https://dvcs.org.au
- Canberra Rape Crisis Centre (24 Hours): 02 6247 2525 https://crcc.org.au
- Canberra Men's Centre: 02 6230 6999 https://www.everyman.org.au
- Legal Aid ACT: 1300 654 314 https://www.legalaidact.org.au
- Women's Legal Service: 02 6257 4377 or 1800 634 669 or https://wlc.org.au/about-us

NEW SOUTH WALES

- NSW Domestic Violence Line—available 24/7: 1800 65 64 63
- NSW Rape Crisis Service: 1800 424 017
- Immigrant Women's Speakout Association: 02 9635 8022 or https://www.speakout.org.au
- Interrelate Family Centres: 1300 839 359
- Legal Aid NSW – Law Access NSW: 1300 888 529

- Gender Centre Transgender and Transsexual People—services for people with gender issues: 02 9569 2366 or https://gendercentre.org.au

NORTHERN TERRITORY

- NTcommunity—online directory of services: https://www.ntcommunity.org.au
- Sexual Assault Referral Centre: https://nt.gov.au/wellbeing/hospitals-health-services/sexual-assault-referral-centres
- Central Australia Women's Legal Service: 1800 684 055 or https://cawls.org.au
- Northern Territory Legal Aid Commission: 1800 019 343

QUEENSLAND

- DV Connect Telephone Service Women's Line—24/7: 1800 811 811 or https://www.dvconnect.org
- DV Connect Men's Line—call 9 am–midnight, 7 days: 1800 600 636
- Sexual Assault Helpline—7.30am–11.30pm, 7 days: 1800 010 120
- Immigrant Women's Support Service: 07 3846 3490 or https://www.iwss.org.au/
- Legal Aid Queensland—Monday to Friday, 8:30 am to 4:30 pm: 1300 65 11 88
- Women's Legal Service Queensland: 1800 957 957 or https://wlsq.org.au/

SOUTH AUSTRALIA

- 24-hour Domestic Violence Crisis Line:
  1800 800 098
- Yarrow Place Sexual Assault Service: 08 8226 8777
  (after hours) or 1800 817 421
- Legal Service Commission: 1300 366 424
- Migrant Women's Support Services: 08 8152 9260
- Women's Legal Service: 08 8231 8929

TASMANIA

- Family Violence Counselling and Support Service:
  1800 608 122
- Sexual Assault Support Service: 1800 697 877
- Women's Legal Service: 1800 682 468
- Legal Aid Tasmania: 1300 366 611
- Migrant Resource Centre: 03 6221 0999

VICTORIA

- Safe Steps Family Violence Response Centre:
  1800 015 188 or web chat https://www.safesteps.
  org.au
- Sexual Assault Crisis Line: 1800 806 292
- Men's Referral Service No to Violence: 1300 766 491
- Victoria Legal Aid: 1300 792 387
- Women's Legal Service Victoria: 1800 133 302

WESTERN AUSTRALIA

- Women's Domestic Violence Helpline: 1800 007 339

- Crisis Care: 1800 199 008
- Sexual Assault Resource Centre: 1800 199 888
- Men's Helpline: 1800 000 599
- Legal Aid WA: 1300 650 579
- Community Legal Centres: https://www.communityle galwa.org.au
- Women's Legal Centre Western Australia (WLCWA): 08 9272 8800 or 1800 625 122

UNITED STATES OF AMERICA

- The National Domestic Violence Hotline: 1.800.799.SAFE (7233) https://www.thehotline.org

UNITED KINGDOM

- 24-hour National Domestic Violence Helpline: 0808 2000 247 or https://www.nationalda-helpline.org.uk
- Domestic or sexual violence and abuse: 0808 802 1414 or https://dsahelpline.org/

EUROPE

- EU-wide number for helplines for victims of violence against women: (116 016) or https://ec.europa.eu/ info/policies/justice-and-fundamental-rights/gender-equality/gender-based-violence/funding-and-aware ness-raising-gender-based-violence_en
- Women against Violence Europe—list of 46 countries' national phone numbers https://ec.europa.eu/justice/ saynostopvaw/helpline.html or the Helplines in

Europe List https://www.coe.int/en/web/istanbul-convention/help-lines

NEW ZEALAND HELPLINES

- Women's Refuge crisis line—free from any phone, 24 hours a day, every day: 0800 733 843 or https://www.govt.nz/browse/law-crime-and-justice/abuse-harassment-domestic-violence/domestic-and-family-violence/

ENDNOTES

INTRODUCTION

1. Anderson, K.M., & Hiersteiner, C. 2008. 'Recovering from childhood sexual abuse: Is a "storybook ending" possible?' *American Journal of Family Therapy*, 36(5), 413–424.
2. Kosenko, K., & Laboy, J. 2014. '"I survived": The content and forms of survival narratives.' *Journal of Loss and Trauma*, 19(6), 497–513. doi:10.1080/15325024.2013.808948.
3. Méndez-Negrete, J. 2013. 'Expressive creativity: Narrative text and creative cultural expressions as a healing praxis.' *Journal of Creativity in Mental Health*, 8(3), 314. doi:10.1080/15401383.2013.821934.
4. Anderson, K. M., Renner, L. M., & Danis, F. S. 2012. 'Recovery: Resilience and growth in the aftermath of domestic violence.' *Violence Against Women,* 18(11), 1279–1299.
5. Carman, M.J., Kay-Lambkin, F. & Burgman, I. 2022. 'Long-Term Recovery from Intimate Partner Violence: Definitions by Australian Women.' *Journal of Family Violence.* https://doi.org/10.1007/s10896-022-00389-3
6. Queensland Domestic and Family Violence Protection Act. 2012. https://www.legislation.qld.gov.au/view/pdf/2017-05-30/act-2012-005
7. The National Council to Reduce Violence against Women and their Children. 2009. Domestic violence laws in Australia. Department of Families, Housing, Community Services, and Indigenous Affairs (FAHCSIA).
8. Australia's National Research Organisation for Women's Safety. 2021. *Defining and responding to coercive control: Policy brief* (ANROWS Insights, 01/2021).
9. Commonwealth of Australia (Department of Social Services). 2022. *National Plan to End Violence against Women and Children 2022-2032: Ending gender-based violence in one generation.* https://www.dss.gov.au/women-programs-ser vices-reducing-violence/the-national-plan-to-end-violence-against-women-and-children-2022-2032
10. Evans, D. I. 2007. *Battle-scars:Long-term effects of prior domestic violence.* Centre for Women's Studies and Gender Research, Melbourne.
11. The National Council to Reduce Violence against Women and their Children (NCRVWC). 2009. *Background paper to Time for Action: The National Council's plan to reduce violence against women and children, 2009–2021.* p. 13. https://www.dss.gov.au/women-programs-services-reducing-violence-national-plan-to-reduce-violence-against-women-and-their-children/back

ground-paper-to-time-for-action-the-national-councils-plan-for-australia-to-reduce-violence-against-women-and-their-children-2009-2021

12. Tually, S., Faulkner, D., Cutler. C., & Slatter, M. 2008. *Women, domestic and family violence and homelessness: A synthesis report.* Flinders University, Flinders Institute for Housing, Urban and Regional Research. http://www.dpmc.gov.au/women/publications-articles/safety-women/women-synthesis-report-HTML.cfm#c

13. Victorian Government, Department of Human Services. 2007. *Family violence risk assessment and risk management framework.* p. 21. http://www.dhs.vic.gov.au/__data/assets/pdf_file/0006/581757/risk-assessment-risk-man agement-framework-2007.pdf

14. The National Council to Reduce Violence against Women and their Children (NCRVWC). 2009. *Background paper to Time for Action: The National Council's plan to reduce violence against women and children, 2009–2021.* https://www.dss.gov.au/women-programs-services-reducing-violence-national-plan-to-reduce-violence-against-women-and-their-children/background-paper-to-time-for-action-the-national-councils-plan-for-australia-to-reduce-violence-against-women-and-their-children-2009-2021

15. Carter, A., Bateson, D., & Vaughan, C. 'Reproductive coercion and abuse in Australia: what do we need to know?' *Sex Health.* 2021 Nov;18(5):436-440. doi: 10.1071/SH21116. PMID: 34731597.

16. 1800 RESPECT. Reproductive abuse. https://www.1800respect.org.au/repro ductive-abuse

17. Gooda, M. 2011. *The Eddie Koiki Mabo Lecture 2011. Strengthening our relationships over lands, territories and resources: the United Nations Declaration on the Rights of Indigenous Peoples.* James Cook University. https://www.jcu.edu.au/__data/assets/pdf_file/0010/789364/jcu_145042.pdf

18. RSPCA Knowledge Base. *Is there a link between domestic violence and animal abuse?* https://kb.rspca.org.au/knowledge-base/is-there-a-link-between-domes tic-violence-and-animal-abuse

19. White Ribbon. 2019. *Signs of an abusive relationship.* https://www.whiterib bon.org.au/understand-domestic-violence/what-is-domestic-violence/signs-abusive-relationship/

20. New Hope for Women. 2019. *Red flags for domestic abuse.* http://www.newhopeforwomen.org/red-flags-for-domestic-abuse

21. Ali, P., McGarry, J., & Dhingra, K. 2016. 'Identifying signs of intimate partner violence.' *Emergency Nurse,* 23(9), 25–29. doi: https://doi.org/10.7748/en.23.9.25.s25.

22. Cleveland Clinic. 2018. *Domestic abuse: How to spot relationship red flags,* 7 June. https://health.clevelandclinic.org/domestic-abuse-how-to-spot-relation ship-red-flags/

23. Women's Domestic Violence Court Advocacy Program (WDVCAP). 2017. *Charmed and Dangerous.* Legal Aid, NSW. http://lacextra.legalaid.nsw.gov.au/PublicationsResourcesService/PublicationImprints/Files/754.pdf

24. World Health Organisation. 2021. *Violence Against Women Factsheet.* 9 March 2021 https://www.who.int/news-room/fact-sheets/detail/violence-against-women

25. National Coalition Against Domestic Violence. 2020. *Domestic violence.* Retrieved from https://assets.speakcdn.com/assets/2497/domestic_violence-20200807093508855.pdf?1596811079991

26. Office for National Statistics. 2022. *Domestic abuse: Findings from the Crime Survey for England and Wales: Year ending November 2022.* https://www.ons.gov.uk/peoplepopulationandcommunity/crimeandjustice/bulletins/domesticabuseinenglandandwalesoverview/november2022

27. European Commission. 2020. *Let's put an end to Violence against Women.* Factsheet, November. https://ec.europa.eu/info/sites/default/files/aid_development_cooperation_fundamental_rights/factsheet_lets_put_an_end_to_violence_against_women_en.pdf

28. Muluneh, M.D., Stulz, V., Francis, L., & Agho, K. 2020. 'Gender Based Violence against Women in Sub-Saharan Africa: A Systematic Review and Meta-Analysis of Cross-Sectional Studies.' *Int J Environ Res Public Health.* Feb 1;17(3):903. doi: 10.3390/ijerph17030903. PMID: 32024080; PMCID: PMC7037605. https://pubmed.ncbi.nlm.nih.gov/32024080/

29. 'Russia's leaders won't deal with a domestic violence epidemic. These women stepped up instead.' *Time.* https://time.com/5942127/russia-domestic-violence-women/

30. Spring, M. 2018. 'Decriminalisation of domestic violence in Russia leads to fall in reported cases.' *The Guardian*, 16 August. https://www.theguardian.com/world/2018/aug/16/decriminalisation-of-domestic-violence-in-russia-leads-to-fall-in-reported-cases

31. Yoshihama, M., Ph.D., Dabby, C., & Luo, S. 2020. *Facts & Stats Report: Domestic Violence in Asian And Pacific Islander Homes*, October. https://www.api-gbv.org/resources/facts-stats-dv-api-homes/

32. Australian Institute of Health and Welfare. 2019. *Family, domestic and sexual violence in Australia: continuing the national story 2019.* Cat. no. FDV 3. Canberra: AIHW https://www.aihw.gov.au/reports/domestic-violence/family-domestic-sexual-violence-australia-2019/contents/summary

33. Smyth, C., Cullen, P., Breckenridge, J., Cortis, N. & Valentine, K. 2021. 'COVID-19 lockdowns, intimate partner violence and coercive control.' *Aust J Soc Issues*, 56: 359-373. https://doi.org/10.1002/ajs4.162

34. Franzway, S., Wendt, S., Moulding, N., Zufferey, C., Chung, D., & Elder, A. 2015. *Gendered violence and citizenship: The complex effects of intimate partner violence on mental health, housing and employment.* University of South Australia, Magill. http://www.unisa.edu.au/PageFiles/71190/Gendered-Violence-and-Citizenship-report.pdf

35. Loxton, D., Dolja-Gore, X., Anderson, A.E., & Townsend, N. 2017. 'Intimate partner violence adversely impacts health over 16 years and across generations: A longitudinal cohort study.' *PLoS ONE,* 12(6): e0178138.

https://journals.plos.org/plosone/article/file?id=10.1371/journal.pone.0178138&type=printable

36. Anderson, K.M., Renner, L.M., & Danis, F.S. 2012. 'Recovery: Resilience and growth in the aftermath of domestic violence.' *Violence Against Women*, 18(11), 1279–1299.

37. Jones, A., & Vetere, A. 2017. '"You just deal with it. You have to when you've got a child": A narrative analysis of mothers' accounts of how they coped, both during an abusive relationship and after leaving.' *Clinical Child Psychology and Psychiatry*, 22(1), 74–89.

38. Parkin, S. J. 2017. *Survival after violence: The post-separation journey of women who have experienced intimate partner violence.* https://ro.ecu.edu.au/theses/2001

39. Noviyanti, L.K., Hamid, A.Y.S., & Daulima, N.H.C. 2019. 'Experience of domestic violence survivor women in searching their life purpose and self-resilience.' *Journal of International Dental & Medical Research*, 12(1), p. 299, viewed 8 June 2019. https://search.ebscohost.com/login.aspx?direct=true&AuthType=athens&db=edo&AN=135783798&site=eds-live

40. The National Council to Reduce Violence against Women and their Children (NCRVWC). 2009. *Background paper to Time for Action: The National Council's plan to reduce violence against women and children, 2009–2021.* p. 13. https://www.dss.gov.au/women-programs-services-reducing-violence-national-plan-to-reduce-violence-against-women-and-their-children/background-paper-to-time-for-action-the-national-councils-plan-for-australia-to-reduce-violence-against-women-and-their-children-2009-2021 ; Department for Planning and Community Development. 2007. *Family violence risk assessment and risk management framework*, Victorian Government, Melbourne, p. 21, viewed 19 September 2011. http://www.dhs.vic.gov.au/__data/assets/pdf_file/0006/581757/risk-assessment-risk-management-framework-2007.pdf

41. Trauma Recovery. 2013. *Phases of Trauma Recovery.* https://trauma-recovery.ca/recovery/phases-of-trauma-recovery/

42. Community Care Division. 2004. *Women's journey away from family violence – Framework and summary.* Victorian Government Department of Human Services, Melbourne. https://www.secasa.com.au/assets/Documents/womens-journey-away-from-family-violence.pdf

3. SURVIVING THE JIGSAW PUZZLE

1. If you are a self-represented litigant, you have the right to have a person attend court with you and support you in certain ways. Such a person is informally known as a McKenzie friend. https://en.wikipedia.org/wiki/McKenzie_friend

5. SURFACING INTO THE SUNLIGHT

1. Swatz, K. 2022. *Forgiveness: Your Health Depends on It.* The Johns Hopkins University.
2. Schumann, K., & Walton, G. M. 2022. 'Rehumanizing the self after victimization: The roles of forgiveness versus revenge.' *Journal of Personality and Social Psychology*, 122(3), 469–492. https://doi.org/10.1037/pspi0000367
3. Schultz, J. 2020. *Forgiveness Therapy: 6+ Techniques to Help Clients Forgive.* Positive Psychology. https://positivepsychology.com/forgiveness-in-therapy/
4. Luskin, F. 2003. *Forgive for Good: A Proven Prescription for Health and Happiness.* Harper One.

8. STUDY: YOUR STEPPING STONE TO BEING YOU

1. *https://www.qtac.edu.au/special-tertiary-admissions-test/#:~:text=The%20Special%20Tertiary%20Admissions%20Test,to%20consider%20for%20their%20courses*

9. OPERATION PHOENIX RISING

1. Domestic violence orders have different names in different places. They are also known as a protection order, domestic violence restraining order, restraining order, family violence intervention order, intervention order, family violence order, domestic violence order, apprehended violence order, apprehended domestic violence order and more.

11. THE IMPACT OF WRITING MY STORY

1. https://www.mayoclinic.org/diseases-conditions/dissociative-disorders/symptoms-causes/syc-20355215

ABOUT BROKEN TO BRILLIANT

Broken to Brilliant is an Australian not-for-profit charity where domestic violence survivors mentor other survivors to re-establish successful lives using the power of story.

When we saw the impact on people's lives of our first three books – the changes made, the hope in their hearts, the joy and gratitude for their new lives – we had to continue to share the brave, resilient and brilliant stories of hope, healing and recovery. There had to be a fourth book.

We applaud each of our authors for sharing their raw, vulnerable and courageous stories. Our hope is that these books will provide you with the tools to take back your power so you can rebuild your life the way you choose. That the words will encourage you to step out of the fog of coercive control. Each step forward is a courageous move toward your new life filled with peace, happiness and achievement.

brokentobrilliant.org

BROKEN TO BRILLIANT

Breaking Free to be You After Domestic Violence – Stories of Strength and Success

ISBN: 978-0-9945714-0-3

Bronze medallist, eLit Book Awards 2017

Author Elite Award – Advice category

'That would never happen to me. I'm too strong. I would walk out.' Those were KC Andrews' thoughts as a trainee nurse listening to a lecture on domestic violence. But when it happened to her, it took years to finally leave.

She has now rebuilt her life from the ashes of a brutal marriage, and along the way met other women who have survived the fog of fear and feelings of worthlessness – and then on the outside, endured the disbelief and bureaucratic bungles of those who should have helped.

But now, each woman's brilliance is emerging once again.

Each one tells her unique story to help readers understand the many different shapes domestic violence can take. And yet, the focus of this book is not on the horror, but the healing. Each woman shares the skills, techniques and attitudes that helped her to shine once again.

This book is for anyone who is living in an abusive relationship, knows someone who is, or has emerged and is looking for a roadmap out of darkness into the light of new beginnings.

TERROR TO TRIUMPH

Rebuilding Your Life After Domestic Violence – Stories of Strength and Success

ISBN: 978-0-9945714-9-6

'People congratulated me when I left my abusive marriage, but I didn't feel like celebrating. I felt loss, grief, shame, anger, resentment, regret, uncertainty, relief and excitement. How can one person feel so many emotions at once? Where could I go for help? Who would understand?'

From these questions the charity Broken to Brilliant was born, where survivors help other survivors rebuild their lives using the power of story.

In *Terror to Triumph*, twelve domestic violence survivors describe the terror they experienced and the additional challenges they encountered from a system that was supposed to help them.

Most importantly, they tell of the practical steps they have taken – physically, emotionally, psychologically and spiritually – to journey from darkness to light and build new lives. They tell of continued recovery, and how they have reclaimed their lives to reach a sense of triumph.

SHATTERED TO SHINING

Journeys of Surviving and Thriving After Domestic Violence – Stories of Strength and Success

ISBN: 9780994571458

'It began with fluttering excitement, joy and a world full of possibilities. There was a slow chiselling away of me. I felt disbelief and foggy confusion, before the ugly reality of abuse dawned on me.'

How do you live through the shattering effects of domestic violence and abuse inflicted by a person you loved, trusted and vowed to spend the rest of your life with? How do you rebuild your life to again be able to value every sunrise and every rainbow, to brightly shine again?

In *Shattered to Shining*, nine women and one male domestic violence survivor describe how they were shattered, as their home became a place where physical and sexual violence, and emotional and psychological control dominated their lives. Through persistence and courage, they have risen above their situation and come out the other side shining with positivity, strength, commitment and empathy for others.

The journey of surviving and thriving is chaotic, emotional, and unique to each person. Each chapter is filled with the shortcuts and tools needed to travel this road of recovery to stand in your new life, with your future brightly shining.

www.ingramcontent.com/pod-product-compliance
Lightning Source LLC
Chambersburg PA
CBHW051108050726
47592CB00002B/723